Forever I Will

Metered Classic Chant Edition

Through-Composed Responsorial Psalms and Gospel Acclamations

December 3, 2023 – November 18, 2024

Year B

Music by Timothy R. Smith

Online Instructional Videos
Visit www.timothyrsmith.com for links to online instructional videos for each of the Responsorial Psalms and Gospel Acclamations. These are helpful in familiarizing cantors and instrumentalists with each piece.

Refrain Melodies for Assembly Worship Aids
To receive pdf of all refrain melodies at no additional charge, send copy of receipt to
forever@timothyrsmith.com

Forever I Will Sing 2024 (Classic Chant Edition)
Responsorial Psalms and Gospel Acclamations
Year B – December 3, 2023 through November 18, 2024

Musical settings by Timothy R. Smith
This songbook © 2023, Timothy R. Smith. Published by TR TUNE, LLC. All rights reserved.
www.timothyrsmith.com
ISBN: 978-1-960532-02-2

All musical settings by Timothy R. Smith. Some settings were previously published by OCP, 5536 NE Hassalo, Portland, OR 97213-3638; as indicated, they are available at www.ocp.org

Also available at www.timothyrsmith.com:
Forever I Will Sing 2024 Metered Keyboard Edition
Forever I Will Sing 2024 Metered Guitar/Vocal Edition

Publisher: TR TUNE, LLC, Waterford, MI   www.timothyrsmith.com
Composer: Timothy R. Smith
Editor: Barbara Bridge
Cover Art: Mary Dudek
                     www.marydudekart.com

We are still developing and refining this format and we welcome any feedback. Please feel free to contact me anytime if you have feedback about any aspect of this publication.

Tim Smith
tim@timothyrsmith.com

Singing the Psalm Settings

Psalm Refrains can be adapted to piano, organ, guitar accompaniment, or even SATB choir. The melodies, rhythms and harmonies are designed to embody the spirit of the text.

Verse Chants are set for solo voice (Cantor) with sustained keyboard or guitar accompaniment.

General Directives for Chanting the Verses

Consider the example below for a discussion of the various musical elements:

In the chanted verses, the music follows the "speech rhythm" of the text, flowing smoothly so that the text is understood and its meaning is clear.

Black notes indicate that all the verses have only one syllable on that note.

Open notes indicate that at least one verse has multiple syllables on the open note. Where there is only one syllable on an open note, the cantor should sing that syllable as though it is a black note–not sustaining that syllable–but maintaining the speech rhythm of the text.

The Right Slash " / " indicates that one phrase ends and a new phrase begins on the same note, with a slight pause at the end of the phrase before the slash. For example, at the end of Verse 2a there is a pause between "creatures;" and "bless" to distinguish between the two phrases.

Braces "{ }" act as repeat signs. For example, at the end of Verse 4a, the right bracket "}" indicates a repeat to the left bracket "{" at 4b. Thus, the cantor connects 4a and 4b to complete the phrase, "they are created, and you renew the face of the earth." The braces in Verse 2a, 2b, and 2c, direct the cantor to connect all three lines: "the earth is full of your creatures; bless the Lord, O my soul! Alleluia!"

Square Brackets "[ ]" indicate a repetition of words or phrases from the original text.

PAGE	SUNDAY	REFRAIN	PSALM REFERENCE
8	First Sunday of Advent	Lord, make us turn to you	Psalm 80:2–3, 15–16, 18–19
10	Immaculate Conception	Sing to the Lord a new song	Psalm 98:1, 2–3ab, 3cd–4
12	Second Sunday of Advent	Lord, let us see your kindness	Psalm 85:9–10, 11–12, 13–14
14	Our Lady of Guadalupe	You are the highest honor of our race	Judith 13:18bcde, 19
16	Third Sunday of Advent	My soul rejoices in my God	Luke 1:46–48, 49–50, 53–54
18	Fourth Sunday of Advent	For ever I will sing	Psalm 89:2-3, 4-5, 27, 29
20	The Nativity of the Lord (Christmas): At the Vigil Mass	Forever I will sing	Psalm 89:4-5, 16-17, 27, 29
22	The Nativity of the Lord (Christmas): At the Mass during the Night	Today is born our savior	Psalm 96:1-2, 2-3, 11-12, 13
24	The Nativity of the Lord (Christmas): At the Mass at Dawn	A light will shine on us this day	Psalm 97:1, 6, 11-12
26	The Nativity of the Lord (Christmas): At the Mass during The Day	All the ends of the earth	Psalm 98:1, 2-3, 3-4, 5-6
28	The Holy Family of Jesus, Mary and Joseph	The Lord remembers his covenant	Psalm 105:1–2, 3–4, 5–6, 8–9
30	The Holy Family of Jesus, Mary and Joseph	Blessed are those who fear the Lord	Psalm 128:1-2, 3, 4-5, 6
32	Mary, Mother of God	May God bless us in his mercy	Psalm 67:2-3, 5, 6, 8
34	The Epiphany of the Lord	Lord, every nation on earth	Psalm 72:1–2, 7–8, 10–11, 12–13
36	Second Sunday in Ordinary Time	Here am I, Lord; I come to do your will	Psalm 40:2, 4, 7–8, 8–9, 10
38	Third Sunday in Ordinary Time	Teach me your ways, O Lord	Psalm 25:4–5, 6–7, 8–9
40	Fourth Sunday in Ordinary Time	If today you hear his voice	Psalm 95:1–2, 6–7, 7–9
42	Fifth Sunday in Ordinary Time	Praise the Lord, who heals	Psalm 147:1–2, 3–4, 5–6
44	Sixth Sunday in Ordinary Time	I turn to you, Lord, in time of trouble	Psalm 32:1–2, 5, 11
46	Ash Wednesday	Be merciful, O Lord,	Psalm 51:3-4, 5-6ab, 12-13, 14 & 17
48	First Sunday of Lent	Your ways, O Lord, are love and truth	Psalm 25:4–5, 6–7, 8–9
50	Second Sunday of Lent	I will walk before the Lord	Psalm 116:10, 15, 16–17, 18–19
52	Third Sunday of Lent	Lord, you have the words	Psalm 19:8, 9, 10, 11
54	RCIA Option: Third Sunday of Lent	If today you hear his voice	Psalm 95:1-2, 6-7, 8-9
56	Fourth Sunday of Lent	Let my tongue be silenced	Psalm 137:1–2, 3, 4–5, 6
58	RCIA Option: Fourth Sunday of Lent	The Lord is my shepherd	Psalm 23:1-3a, 3b-4, 5, 6
60	Fifth Sunday of Lent	Create a clean heart in me, O God	Psalm 51:3–4, 12–13, 14–15
62	RCIA Option: Fifth Sunday of Lent	With the Lord there is mercy	Psalm 130:1-2, 3-4, 5-6, 7-8
64	Palm Sunday of the Passion of the Lord	My God, my God	Psalm 22:8-9, 17-18, 19-20, 23-24
66	Thursday of the Lord's Supper: At the Evening Mass	Our blessing cup is a communion	Psalm 116:12-13, 15-16bc, 17-18
68	Friday of the Passion of the Lord (Good Friday)	Father, into your hands	Psalm 31:2, 6, 12-13, 15-16, 17, 25
70	The Easter Vigil in the Holy Night	Lord, send out your Spirit	24, 35
71	The Easter Vigil in the Holy Night	The earth is full of the goodness	Psalm 33:4-5, 6-7, 12-13, 20 & 22
72	The Easter Vigil in the Holy Night	You are my inheritance	Psalm 16:5, 8, 9-10, 11
74	The Easter Vigil in the Holy Night	Let us sing to the Lord	Exodus 15:1-2, 3-4, 5-6, 17-18
76	The Easter Vigil in the Holy Night	I will praise you Lord	Psalm 30:2, 4, 5-6, 11-12, 13
77	The Easter Vigil in the Holy Night	You will draw water	Isaiah 12:2-3, 4bcd, 5-6
78	The Easter Vigil in the Holy Night	Lord, you have the words	Psalm 19:8, 9, 10, 11
80	The Easter Vigil in the Holy Night	Like a deer	Psalm 42:3, 5; 43:3, 4
81	The Easter Vigil in the Holy Night	You will draw water	Isaiah 12:2-3, 4bcd, 5-6
82	The Easter Vigil in the Holy Night	Create a clean heart in me, O God	Psalm 51:12-13, 14-15, 18-19
83	The Easter Vigil Gospel Acclamation	Alleluia	Psalm 118:1-2, 16-17, 22-23
84	Easter Sunday: Mass during the Day	This is the day	Psalm 118:1-2, 16-17, 22-23
86	Second Sunday of Easter (or Sunday of Divine Mercy)	Give thanks to the Lord	Psalm 118:2-4, 13-15, 22-24
88	Third Sunday of Easter	Lord, let your face shine on us	Psalm 4:2, 4, 7–8, 9

PAGE	SUNDAY	REFRAIN	PSALM REFERENCE
90	Fourth Sunday of Easter	The stone rejected by the builders	Psalm 118:1, 8–9, 21–23, 26, 28, 29
92	Fifth Sunday of Easter	I will praise you, Lord, in the assembly	Psalm 22:26–27, 28, 30, 31–32
94	Sixth Sunday of Easter	The Lord has revealed to the nations	Psalm 98:1, 2–3, 3–4
96	The Ascension of the Lord	God mounts his throne	Psalm 47:2-3, 6-7, 8-9
98	Seventh Sunday of Easter	The Lord has set his throne in heaven.	Psalm 103:1–2, 11–12, 19–20
100	Pentecost Sunday: Extended Vigil Mass	Blessed the people the Lord has chose	Psalm 33:10-11, 12-13, 14-15
102	Pentecost Sunday: Extended Vigil Mass	Glory and praise forever	Daniel 3:52, 53, 54, 55, 56
104	Pentecost Sunday: Extended Vigil Mass	Lord, you have the words	Psalm 19:8, 9, 10, 11
106	Pentecost Sunday: Extended Vigil Mass	Give thanks to the Lord	Psalm 107:2-3, 4-5, 6-7, 8-9
108	Pentecost Sunday: Extended Vigil Mass	Lord, send out your Spirit	Psalm 104:1-2, 24 & 35, 27-28, 29-30
110	Pentecost Sunday: At the Mass during the Day	Lord, send out your Spirit	Psalm 104:1, 24, 29-30, 31, 34
112	The Most Holy Trinity	Blessed the people the Lord has chose	Psalm 33:4–5, 6, 9, 18–19, 20, 22
114	The Most Holy Body and Blood of Christ (Corpus Christi)	I will take the cup of salvation	Psalm 116:12–13, 15–16, 17–18
116	10th Sunday in Ordinary Time	With the Lord there is mercy	Psalm 130:1-2, 3-4, 5-6, 7-8
118	11th Sunday in Ordinary Time	Lord, it is good to give thanks to you	Psalm 92:2–3, 13–14, 15–16
120	12th Sunday in Ordinary Time	Give thanks to the Lord	Psalm 107:23-24, 25-26, 28-29, 30-31
122	13th Sunday in Ordinary Time	I will praise you, Lord	Psalm 30:2, 4, 5–6, 11, 12, 13
124	14th Sunday in Ordinary Time	Our eyes are fixed on the Lord	Psalm 123:1–2, 2, 3–4
126	15th Sunday in Ordinary Time	Lord, let us see your kindness	Psalm 85:9–10, 11–12, 13–14
128	16th Sunday in Ordinary Time	The Lord is my shepherd	Psalm 23:1–3, 3–4, 5, 6
130	17th Sunday in Ordinary Time	The hand of the Lord feeds us	Psalm 145:10–11, 15–16, 17–18
132	18th Sunday in Ordinary Time	The Lord gave them bread from heaven	Psalm 78:3–4, 23–24, 25, 54
134	19th Sunday in Ordinary Time	Taste and see the goodness of the Lord	Psalm 34:2–3, 4–5, 6–7, 8–9
136	The Assumption of the Blessed Virgin Mary: At the Vigil Mass	Lord, go up to your place of rest	Psalm 132:6-7, 9-10, 13-14
138	The Assumption of the Blessed Virgin Mary: At the Mass during the Day	The queen stands at your right hand	Psalm 45:10, 11, 12, 16
140	20th Sunday in Ordinary Time	Taste and see the goodness of the Lord	Psalm 34:2-3, 4-5, 6-7
142	21st Sunday in Ordinary Time	Taste and see the goodness of the Lord	Psalm 34:2–3, 16–17, 18–19, 20–21
144	22nd Sunday in Ordinary Time	The one who does justice	Psalm 15:2–3, 3–4, 4–5
146	23rd Sunday in Ordinary Time	Praise the Lord, my soul!	Psalm 146:6-7, 8–9, 9–10
148	24th Sunday in Ordinary Time	I will walk before the Lord	Psalm 116:1–2, 3–4, 5–6, 8–9
150	25th Sunday in Ordinary Time	The Lord upholds my life	Psalm 54:3–4, 5, 6 & 8
152	26th Sunday in Ordinary Time	The precepts of the Lord	Psalm 19:8, 10, 12–13, 14
154	27th Sunday in Ordinary Time	May the Lord bless us all the days	Psalm 128:1–2, 3, 4–5, 6
156	28th Sunday in Ordinary Time	Fill us with your love, O Lord	Psalm 90:12–13, 14–15, 16–17
158	29th Sunday in Ordinary Time	Lord, let your mercy be on us	Psalm 33:4–5, 18–19, 20, 22
160	30th Sunday in Ordinary Time	The Lord has done great things for us	Psalm 126:1–2, 2–3, 4–5, 6
162	All Saints	Lord, this is the people	Psalm 24:1bc-2, 3-4ab, 5-6
164	31st Sunday in Ordinary Time	I love you, Lord, my strength	Psalm 18:2–3, 3–4, 47, 51
166	32nd Sunday in Ordinary Time	Praise the Lord, my soul	Psalm 146:7, 8–9, 9–10
168	33rd Sunday in Ordinary Time	You are my inheritance, O Lord	Psalm 16:5, 8, 9–10, 11
170	Our Lord Jesus Christ, King of the Universe	The Lord is king; he is robed in majesty	Psalm 93:1, 1–2, 5
172	Thanksgiving Day	Blessed be the name of the Lord	Psalm 113:1-2, 3-4, 5-6, 7-8
174	Rite Of Entrance into the Order of Catechumens	Blessed the people the Lord has chose	Psalm 33:4-5, 12-13, 18-19, 20 & 22
176	Selected Psalm for Weddings	Blessed are those who fear the Lord	Psalm 128:1-2, 3, 4-5
177	Selected Psalm for Funerals	The Lord is kind and merciful	18
178	Selected Common (Seasonal) Psalm for Ordinary Time	The Lord is my light and my salvation	Psalm 27:1, 4, 13-14

Scriptural Index

Page	Scripture Reference
102	Daniel 3:52, 53, 54, 55, 56
74	Exodus 15:1-2, 3-4, 5-6, 17-18
77	Isaiah 12:2-3, 4bcd, 5-6
81	Isaiah 12:2-3, 4bcd, 5-6
14	Judith 13:18bcde, 19
16	Luke 1:46–48, 49–50, 53–54
88	Psalm 4:2, 4, 7–8, 9
144	Psalm 15:2–3, 3–4, 4–5
72	Psalm 16:5, 8, 9-10, 11
168	Psalm 16:5, 8, 9–10, 11
164	Psalm 18:2–3, 3–4, 47, 51
152	Psalm 19:8, 10, 12–13, 14
52	Psalm 19:8, 9, 10, 11
78	Psalm 19:8, 9, 10, 11
104	Psalm 19:8, 9, 10, 11
92	Psalm 22:26–27, 28, 30, 31–32
64	Psalm 22:8-9, 17-18, 19-20, 23-24
58	Psalm 23:1-3a, 3b-4, 5, 6
128	Psalm 23:1–3, 3–4, 5, 6
162	Psalm 24:1bc-2, 3-4ab, 5-6
38	Psalm 25:4–5, 6–7, 8–9
48	Psalm 25:4–5, 6–7, 8–9
178	Psalm 27:1, 4, 13-14
76	Psalm 30:2, 4, 5-6, 11-12, 13
122	Psalm 30:2, 4, 5–6, 11, 12, 13
68	Psalm 31:2, 6, 12-13, 15-16, 17, 25
44	Psalm 32:1–2, 5, 11
100	Psalm 33:10-11, 12-13, 14-15
174	Psalm 33:4-5, 12-13, 18-19, 20 & 22
71	Psalm 33:4-5, 6-7, 12-13, 20 & 22
158	Psalm 33:4–5, 18–19, 20, 22
112	Psalm 33:4–5, 6, 9, 18–19, 20, 22
140	Psalm 34:2-3, 4-5, 6-7
142	Psalm 34:2–3, 16–17, 18–19, 20–21
134	Psalm 34:2–3, 4–5, 6–7, 8–9
36	Psalm 40:2, 4, 7–8, 8–9, 10
80	Psalm 42:3, 5; 43:3, 4
138	Psalm 45:10, 11, 12, 16
96	Psalm 47:2-3, 6-7, 8-9
82	Psalm 51:12-13, 14-15, 18-19
46	Psalm 51:3-4, 5-6ab, 12-13, 14 & 17
60	Psalm 51:3–4, 12–13, 14–15
150	Psalm 54:3–4, 5, 6 & 8
32	Psalm 67:2–3, 5, 6, 8
34	Psalm 72:1–2, 7–8, 10–11, 12–13
132	Psalm 78:3–4, 23–24, 25, 54

Page	Scripture Reference
8	Psalm 80:2–3, 15–16, 18–19
12	Psalm 85:9–10, 11–12, 13–14
126	Psalm 85:9–10, 11–12, 13–14
18	Psalm 89:2-3, 4-5, 27, 29
20	Psalm 89:4-5, 16-17, 27, 29
156	Psalm 90:12–13, 14–15, 16–17
118	Psalm 92:2–3, 13–14, 15–16
170	Psalm 93:1, 1–2, 5
54	Psalm 95:1-2, 6-7, 8-9
40	Psalm 95:1–2, 6–7, 7–9
22	Psalm 96:1-2, 2-3, 11-12, 13
24	Psalm 97:1, 6, 11-12
26	Psalm 98:1, 2-3, 3-4, 5-6
94	Psalm 98:1, 2–3, 3–4
10	Psalm 98:1, 2–3ab, 3cd–4
98	Psalm 103:1–2, 11–12, 19–20
177	Psalm 103:8 & 10, 13-14, 15-16, 17-18
108	Psalm 104:1-2, 24 & 35, 27-28, 29-30
70	Psalm 104:1–2, 5-6, 10, 12, 13-14, 24, 35
110	Psalm 104:1, 24, 29-30, 31, 34
28	Psalm 105:1–2, 3–4, 5–6, 8–9
106	Psalm 107:2-3, 4-5, 6-7, 8-9
120	Psalm 107:23-24, 25-26, 28-29, 30-31
172	Psalm 113:1–2, 3–4, 5–6, 7–8
148	Psalm 116:1–2, 3–4, 5–6, 8–9
50	Psalm 116:10, 15, 16–17, 18–19
66	Psalm 116:12-13, 15-16bc, 17-18
114	Psalm 116:12–13, 15–16, 17–18
83	Psalm 118:1-2, 16-17, 22-23
84	Psalm 118:1-2, 16-17, 22-23
90	Psalm 118:1, 8–9, 21–23, 26, 28, 29
86	Psalm 118:2-4, 13-15, 22-24
124	Psalm 123:1–2, 2, 3–4
160	Psalm 126:1–2, 2–3, 4–5, 6
176	Psalm 128:1-2, 3, 4-5
30	Psalm 128:1-2, 3, 4-5, 6
154	Psalm 128:1–2, 3, 4–5, 6
62	Psalm 130:1-2, 3-4, 5-6, 7-8
116	Psalm 130:1-2, 3-4, 5-6, 7-8
136	Psalm 132:6-7, 9-10, 13-14
56	Psalm 137:1–2, 3, 4–5, 6
130	Psalm 145:10–11, 15–16, 17–18
146	Psalm 146:6-7, 8–9, 9–10
166	Psalm 146:7, 8–9, 9–10
42	Psalm 147:1–2, 3–4, 5–6

Refrain Index

Page	Refrain
24	A light will shine on us this day
26	All the ends of the earth
83	Alleluia
46	Be merciful, O Lord,
30	Blessed are those who fear the Lord
176	Blessed are those who fear the Lord
172	Blessed be the name of the Lord
112	Blessed the people the Lord has chosen
174	Blessed the people the Lord has chosen
100	Blessed the people the Lord has chosen
60	Create a clean heart in me, O God
82	Create a clean heart in me, O God
68	Father, into your hands
156	Fill us with your love, O Lord
18	For ever I will sing
20	Forever I will sing
86	Give thanks to the Lord
106	Give thanks to the Lord
120	Give thanks to the Lord
102	Glory and praise forever
96	God mounts his throne
36	Here am I, Lord; I come to do your will
164	I love you, Lord, my strength
44	I turn to you, Lord, in time of trouble
76	I will praise you Lord
122	I will praise you, Lord
92	I will praise you, Lord, in the assembly
114	I will take the cup of salvation
50	I will walk before the Lord
148	I will walk before the Lord
40	If today you hear his voice
54	If today you hear his voice
56	Let my tongue be silenced
74	Let us sing to the Lord
80	Like a deer
34	Lord, every nation on earth
136	Lord, go up to your place of rest
118	Lord, it is good to give thanks to you
12	Lord, let us see your kindness
126	Lord, let us see your kindness
88	Lord, let your face shine on us
158	Lord, let your mercy be on us
8	Lord, make us turn to you
70	Lord, send out your Spirit
108	Lord, send out your Spirit
110	Lord, send out your Spirit

Page	Refrain
162	Lord, this is the people
52	Lord, you have the words
78	Lord, you have the words
104	Lord, you have the words
32	May God bless us in his mercy
154	May the Lord bless us all the days
64	My God, my God
16	My soul rejoices in my God
66	Our blessing cup is a communion
124	Our eyes are fixed on the Lord
166	Praise the Lord, my soul
146	Praise the Lord, my soul!
42	Praise the Lord, who heals
10	Sing to the Lord a new song
134	Taste and see the goodness of the Lord
140	Taste and see the goodness of the Lord
142	Taste and see the goodness of the Lord
38	Teach me your ways, O Lord
71	The earth is full of the goodness
130	The hand of the Lord feeds us
132	The Lord gave them bread from heaven
160	The Lord has done great things for us
94	The Lord has revealed to the nations
98	The Lord has set his throne in heaven.
177	The Lord is kind and merciful
170	The Lord is king; he is robed in majesty
178	The Lord is my light and my salvation
58	The Lord is my shepherd
128	The Lord is my shepherd
28	The Lord remembers his covenant
150	The Lord upholds my life
144	The one who does justice
152	The precepts of the Lord
138	The queen stands at your right hand
90	The stone rejected by the builders
84	This is the day
22	Today is born our savior
62	With the Lord there is mercy
116	With the Lord there is mercy
72	You are my inheritance
168	You are my inheritance, O Lord
14	You are the highest honor of our race
77	You will draw water
81	You will draw water
48	Your ways, O Lord, are love and truth

First Sunday of Advent

December 3

Gospel Acclamation: cf. Psalm 85:8

Acclamation: (Keyboard/SATB) NO. III

(M.M. ♩ = c. 160)

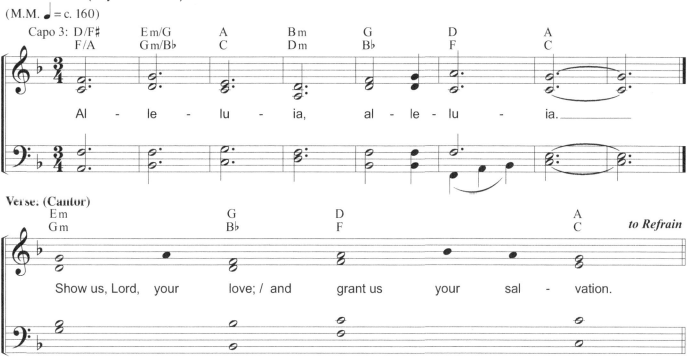

Al - le - lu - ia, al - le - lu - ia.

Verse. (Cantor)

Show us, Lord, your love; / and grant us your sal - vation.

to Refrain

The Immaculate Conception of the Blessed Virgin Mary

January 7

(M.M. ♪ = c. 190)

Psalm 98:1, 2-3ab, 3cd-4

Gospel Acclamation: Luke 1:28

Acclamation: (Keyboard/SATB) NO. IV

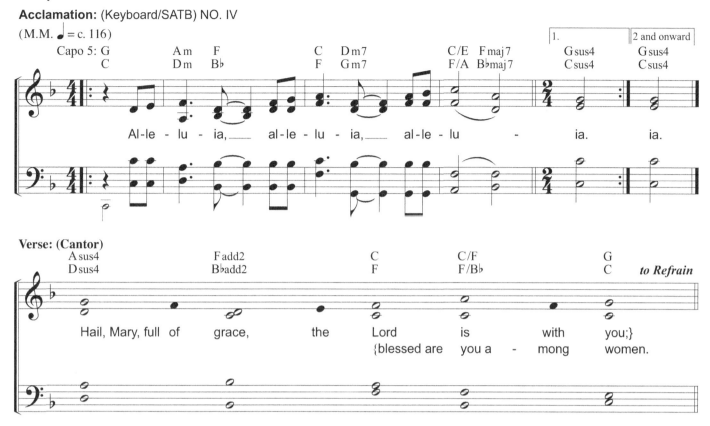

Verse: (Cantor)

Second Sunday of Advent

December 10

Gospel Acclamation: Luke 3:4, 6

Acclamation: (Keyboard/SATB) NO. I

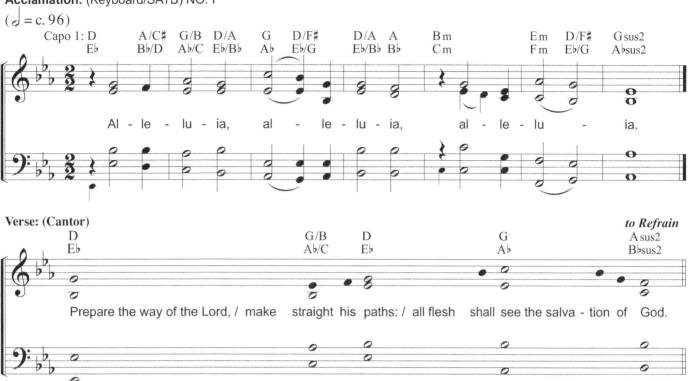

Al - le - lu - ia, al - le - lu - ia, al - le - lu - ia.

Verse: (Cantor)   *to Refrain*

Prepare the way of the Lord, / make straight his paths: / all flesh shall see the salva - tion of God.

Our Lady of Guadalupe

January 7

Judith 13:18bcde, 19

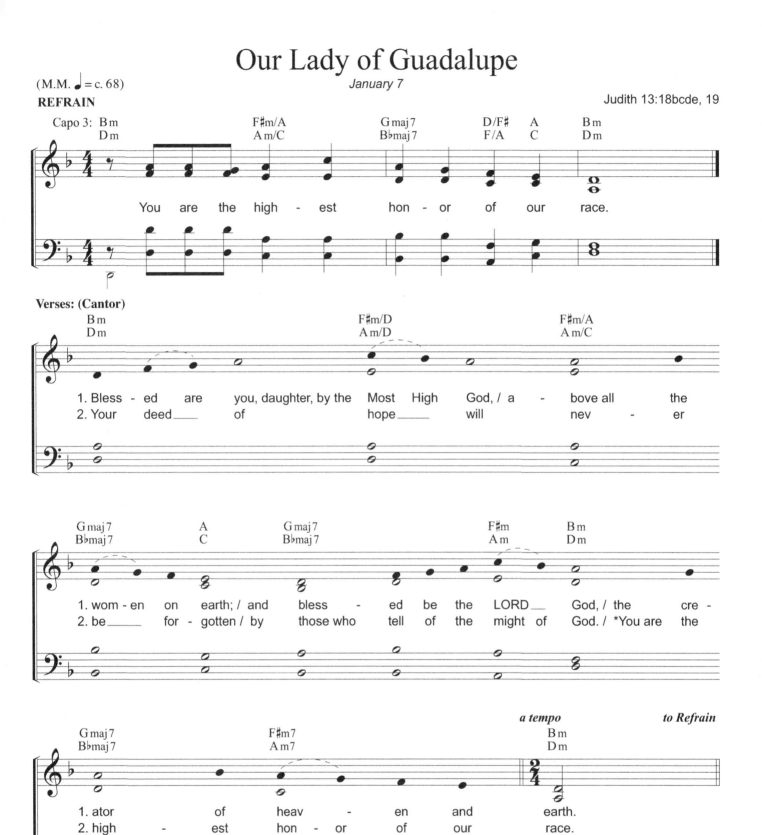

* *Added line*

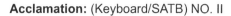

Gospel Acclamation:

Acclamation: (Keyboard/SATB) NO. II

(M.M. ♩ = c. 130)

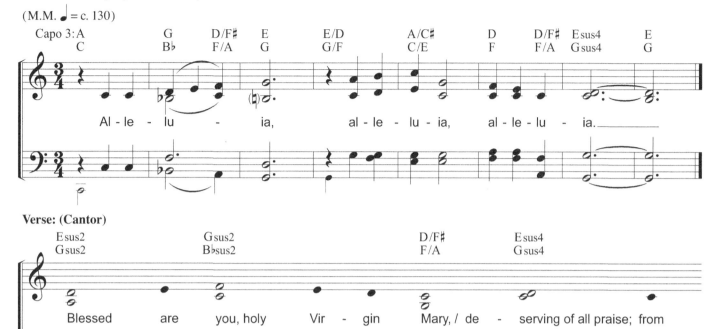

Verse: (Cantor)

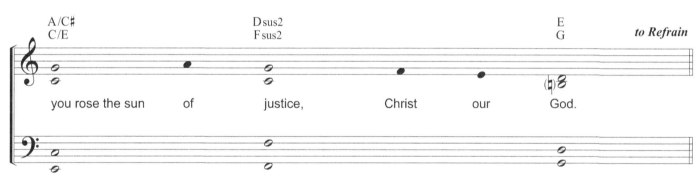

Third Sunday of Advent

December 17

Luke 1:46–48, 49–50, 53–54

Gospel Acclamation: Isaiah 61:1 (cited in Luke 4:18)

Acclamation: (Keyboard/SATB) NO. IV

Al - le - lu - ia,___ al - le - lu - ia,___ al - le - lu - ia. ia.

Verse: (Cantor)

The Spirit of the Lord is up - on me, / because he has a - nointed me to bring glad tidings to the poor.

Fourth Sunday of Advent

December 24

Gospel Acclamation: Luke 1:38

Acclamation: (Keyboard/SATB) NO. II

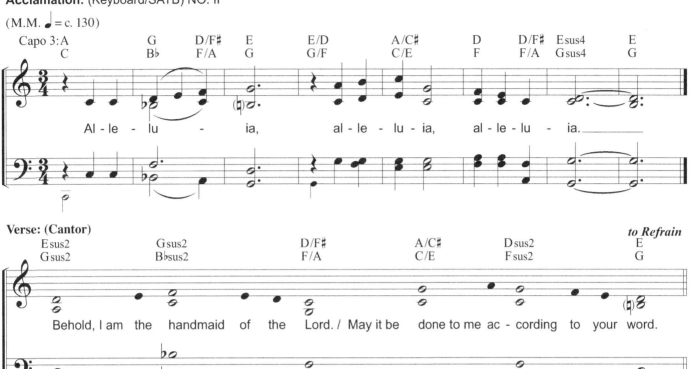

Al - le - lu - ia, al - le - lu - ia, al - le - lu - ia.____

Verse: (Cantor)

to Refrain

Behold, I am the handmaid of the Lord. / May it be done to me ac - cording to your word.

Music © 2014, Timothy R. Smith. Published by TR TUNE, LLC. All rights reserved.

19

The Nativity of The Lord (Christmas): At the Vigil Mass

January 7

(M.M. ♩ = c. 90)

Psalm 89:4-5, 16-17, 27, 29

REFRAIN

For ev - er I will sing the good - ness of the Lord. For ev - er I will sing the good - ness of the Lord.

Verses: (Cantor)

1. I have made a covenant with my chosen one, / I have sworn to David my servant: / Forever will I con - firm your pos - terity / and establish your throne for all gen - er - a - tions.
2. Blessed the people who know the joy - ful shout; / in the light of your countenance, O LORD, they walk. / At your name they re - joice all the day, / and through your justice they are ex - al - ted.
3. He shall say of me, "You are my father, / my God, the rock, my savior." / Forever I will main - tain my kind - ness toward him, / and my covenant with him stands firm.

Gospel Acclamation:

Acclamation: (Keyboard/SATB) NO. V

Verse: (Cantor)

to Refrain

Tomorrow the wickedness of the earth will be de - stroyed: the Savior of the world will reign ov - er us.

The Nativity of the Lord (Christmas): At the Mass during the Night

January 7

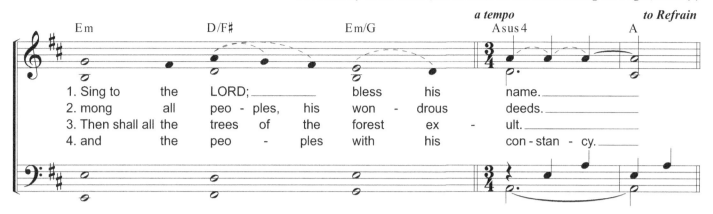

1. Sing to the LORD; _____ bless his name._____
2. mong all peo - ples, his won - drous deeds._____
3. Then shall all the trees of the forest ex - ult._____
4. and the peo - ples with his con - stan - cy._____

Gospel Acclamation: Luke 2:10-11

Acclamation: (Keyboard/SATB) NO. V

Al - le - lu - ia, al - le - lu - ia. Al - le - lu - ia, al - le - lu - ia.

Verse: (Cantor)

I proclaim to you good news of great joy: / to - day a Sav - ior is born for us, Christ the Lord.

The Nativity of the Lord (Christmas): At the Mass at Dawn

January 7

Psalm 97:1, 6, 11-12

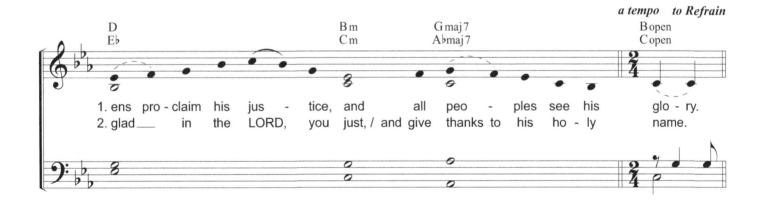

Gospel Acclamation: Luke 2:14

Acclamation: (Keyboard/SATB) NO. V

(M.M. ♪ = c. 150)

Al - le-lu - ia, al-le-lu - ia. Al - le-lu - ia, al - le-lu - ia.

Verse: (Cantor)

to Refrain

Glory to God __ in the highest, / and on earth peace to those on whom his fav - or rests.

The Nativity of the Lord (Christmas): At the Mass during the Day

January 7

Gospel Acclamation:

Acclamation: (Keyboard/SATB) NO. V

The Holy Family of Jesus, Mary and Joseph

Optional year B
December 31

Psalm 105:1–2, 3–4, 5–6, 8–9

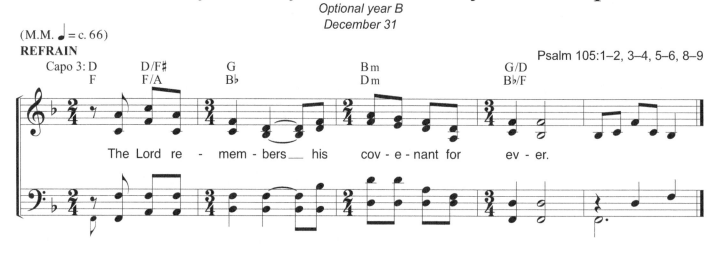

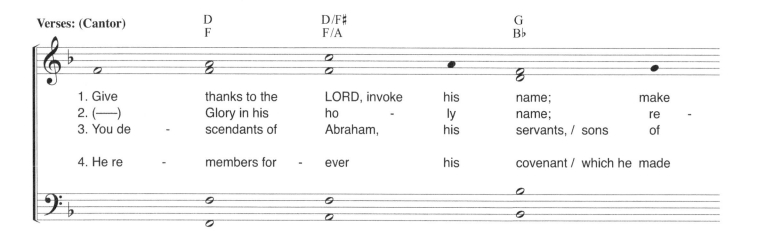

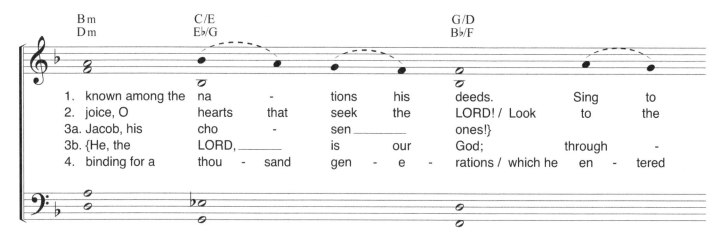

For alternate **Responsorial Psalm** and **Gospel Acclamation Verse,** see pp.30-31. (Setting for Years ABC)

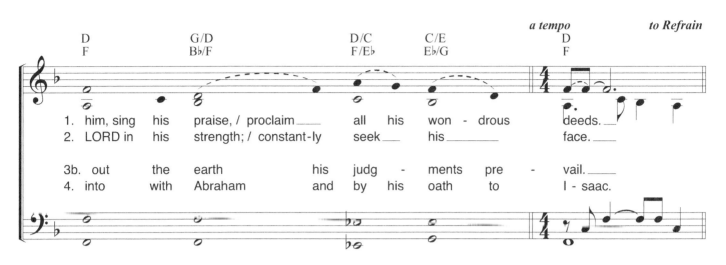

1. him, sing his praise, / proclaim all his won - drous deeds.
2. LORD in his strength; / constant-ly seek his face.

3b. out the earth his judg - ments pre - vail.
4. into with Abraham and by his oath to I - saac.

Gospel Acclamation: Hebrew 1:1-2
Acclamation: (Keyboard/SATB) NO. III
(M.M. ♩ = c. 160)

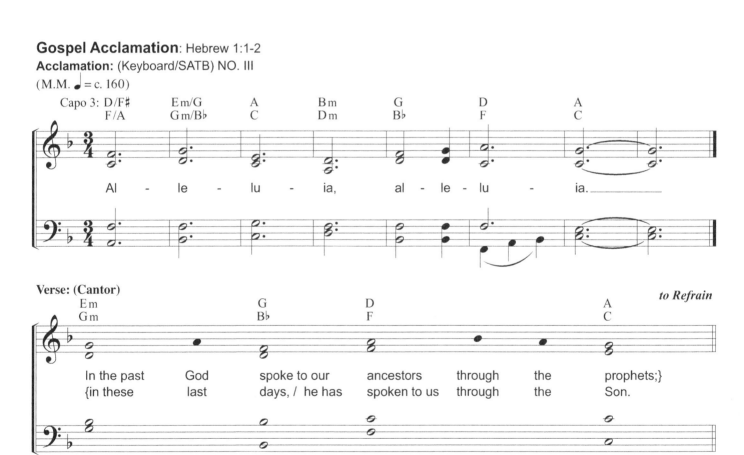

Al - le - lu - ia, al - le - lu - ia.

Verse: (Cantor)

In the past God spoke to our ancestors through the prophets;}
{in these last days, / he has spoken to us through the Son.

The Holy Family of Jesus, Mary and Joseph

December 31

Psalm 128:1-2, 3, 4-5

Alternate Response: "See how the Lord blesses those who fear him."

For alternate **Responsorial Psalms** for weddings, see *Lectionary for the Mass, Second Typical Edition* #803.

Gospel Acclamation: Col 3: 15A, 16A
Acclamation: (Keyboard/SATB) NO. III

Al - le - lu - ia, al - le - lu - ia. _____

Verse: (Cantor)

to Refrain

Let the peace of Christ con - trol your hearts;}
{let the word of Christ dwell in you richly.

Solemnity of Mary, the Holy Mother of God

January 7

Gospel Acclamation: Hebrews 1:1-2

Acclamation: (Keyboard/SATB) NO. I

Verse: (Cantor)

Music: *Mass of the Sacred Heart*; Timothy R. Smith, © 2007, 2010, Timothy R. Smith. Published by OCP. All rights reserved.

The Epiphany of the Lord

January 7

Psalm 72:1-2, 7-8, 10-11, 12-13

Gospel Acclamation: Matthew 2:2

Acclamation: (Keyboard/SATB) NO. II

(M.M. ♩ = c. 130)

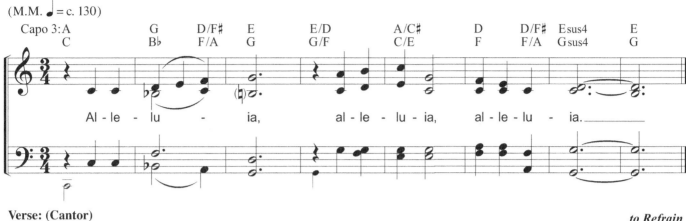

Al - le - lu - ia, al - le - lu - ia, al - le - lu - ia.

Verse: (Cantor)   *to Refrain*

We saw his star at its rising / and have come to do____ him homage.

Music © 2014, Timothy R. Smith. Published by TR TUNE, LLC. All rights reserved.

Second Sunday in Ordinary Time

January 14

Psalm 40:2, 4, 7-8, 8-9, 10

Gospel Acclamation: John 1:41, 17b

Acclamation: (Keyboard/SATB) NO. V

Al - le - lu - ia, al - le - lu - ia. Al - le - lu - ia, al - le - lu - ia.

Verse: (Cantor) *to Refrain*

We have found the Mes - si - ah: Je - sus Christ, who brings us truth and grace.

Third Sunday in Ordinary Time

January 21

($\quad$ = c. 70)

REFRAIN

Psalm 25:4-5, 6-7, 8-9

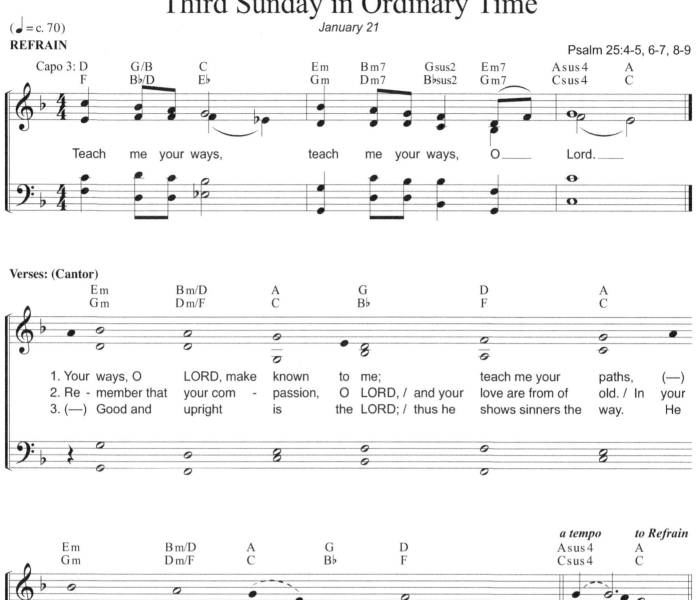

Verses: (Cantor)

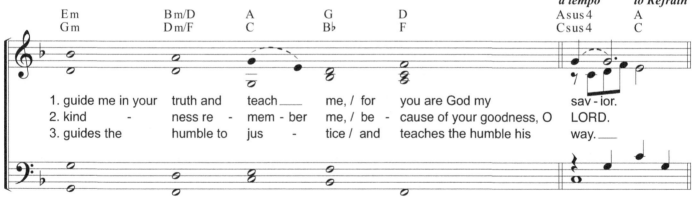

Gospel Acclamation: Mark 1:15
Acclamation: (Keyboard/SATB) NO. III

Al - le - lu - ia, al - le - lu - ia.___

Verse: (Cantor)

The kingdom of God is at hand. / Re - pent and believe in the Gospel.

Fourth Sunday in Ordinary Time

January 28

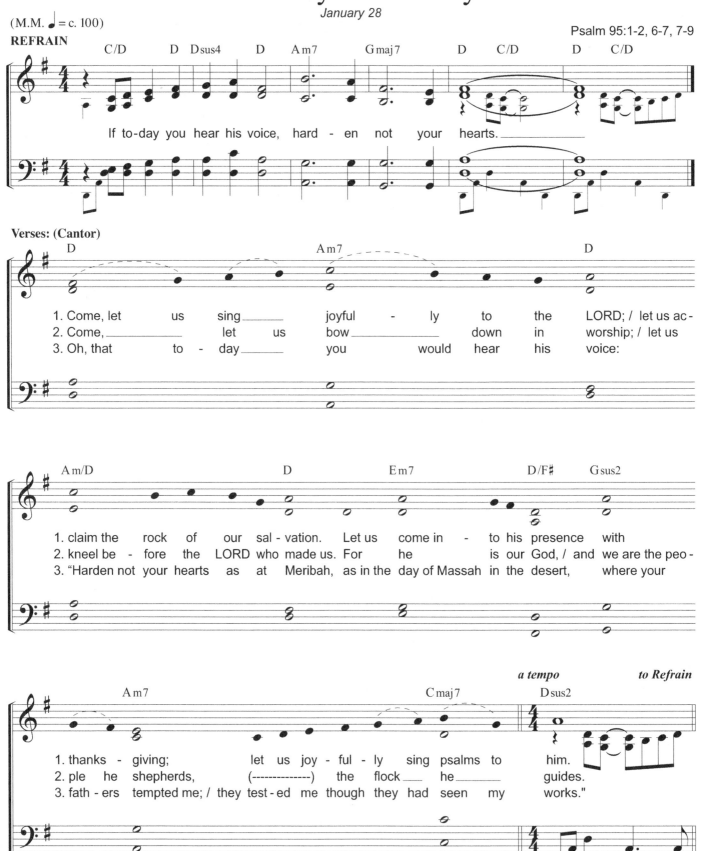

Gospel Acclamation: Matthew 4:16

Acclamation: (Keyboard/SATB) NO. IV

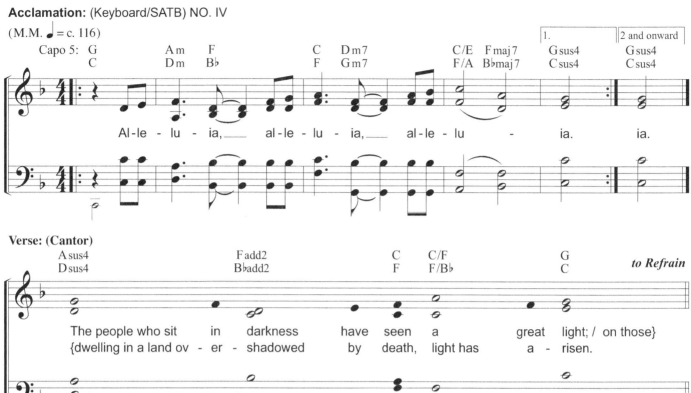

Verse: (Cantor)

The people who sit in darkness have seen a great light; / on those}
{dwelling in a land ov - er - shadowed by death, light has a - risen.

Fifth Sunday in Ordinary Time

February 4

(M.M. ♩ = c. 94)

REFRAIN [or: Alleluia]

Psalm 147:1–2, 3–4, 5–6

Verses: (Cantor)

1. Praise the LORD, for he is good; / sing praise to our God, for he is gracious; / it is fit - ting to praise him. The LORD rebuilds Jer - u - salem; / the dis - persed of Isra - el he gath - ers.

2. He heals the bro - ken - heart - ed and binds up their wounds. He tells the num - ber of the stars; / he calls each by name.

3. Great is our Lord and migh - ty in power; / to his wis - dom there is no limit. / The LORD sustains the low - ly; / the wicked he casts to the ground.

Gospel Acclamation: Matthew 8:17

Acclamation: (Keyboard/SATB) NO. I

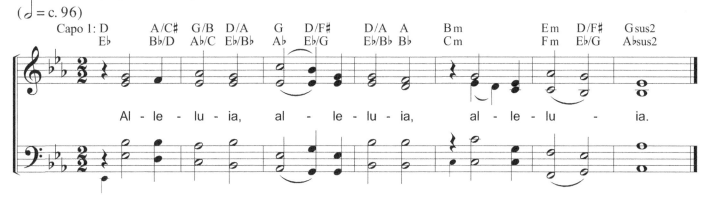

Al - le - lu - ia, al - le - lu - ia, al - le - lu - ia.

Verse: (Cantor)

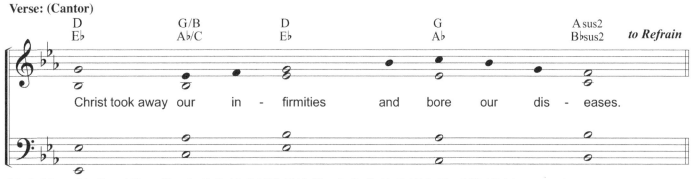

Christ took away our in - firmities and bore our dis - eases.

Sixth Sunday in Ordinary Time

February 11

Psalm 32:1-2, 5, 11

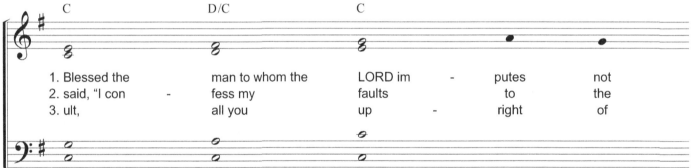

Gospel Acclamation: Luke 7:16

Acclamation: (Keyboard/SATB) NO. III

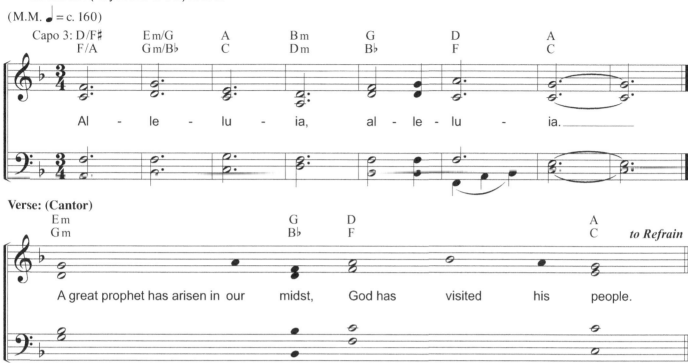

Al - le - lu - ia, al - le - lu - ia.

Verse: (Cantor)

A great prophet has arisen in our midst, God has visited his people.

Ash Wednesday

February 14

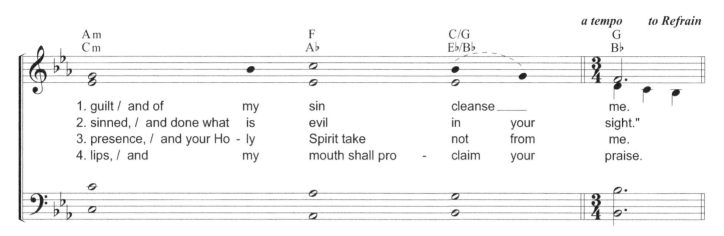

1. guilt / and of my sin cleanse_____ me.
2. sinned, / and done what is evil in your sight."
3. presence, / and your Ho - ly Spirit take not from me.
4. lips, / and my mouth shall pro - claim your praise.

Gospel Acclamation: Psalm 95:8

Acclamation: (Keyboard/SATB) NO. VII

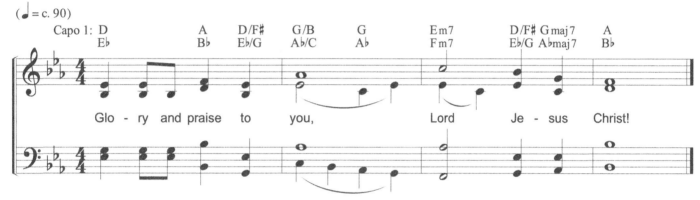

Glo - ry and praise to you, Lord Je - sus Christ!

Verse: (Cantor) *to Refrain*

If today you hear his voice, / hard - en not your_____ hearts.

First Sunday of Lent

February 18

Psalm 25:4–5, 6–7, 8–9

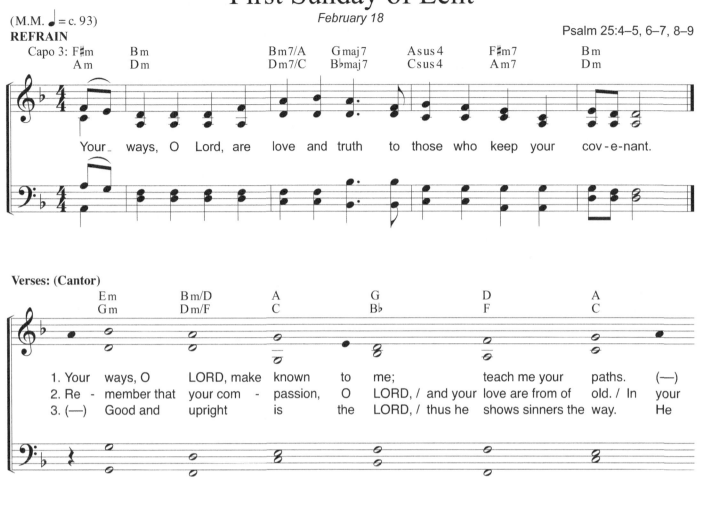

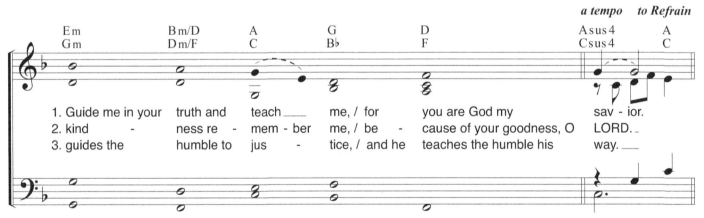

Gospel Acclamation: Matthew 4:4b

Acclamation: (Keyboard/SATB) NO. VI

(M.M. ♩ = c. 104)

Praise to you, Lord Je - sus Christ, King of end - less glo - ry!

Verse: (Cantor)   *to Refrain*

One does not live on bread a - lone, / but on every word that comes forth from the mouth of God.

Second Sunday of Lent

February 25

Gospel Acclamation: Matthew 17:5

Acclamation: (Keyboard/SATB) NO. VII

Glo - ry and praise to you, Lord Je - sus Christ!

Verse: (Cantor) *to Refrain*

From the shining cloud the Father's voice is heard: / This is my belov - ed Son, lis - ten to him.

Music: *Mass of the Sacred Heart*; Timothy R. Smith, © 2007, 2010, Timothy R. Smith. Published by OCP. All rights reserved.

Third Sunday of Lent

March 3

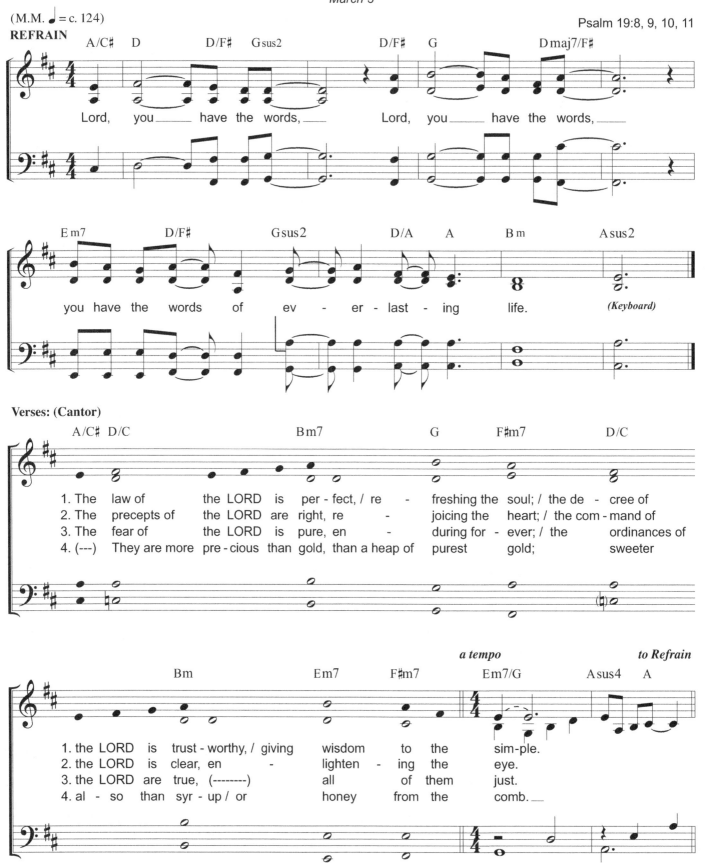

Music © 2007, Timothy R. Smith. Published by OCP. All rights reserved.
Through composed octavo Ed. 30100583 available at www.ocp.org.

Gospel Acclamation: John 3:16

Acclamation: (Keyboard/SATB) NO. VI

(M.M. ♩ = c. 104)

Praise to you, Lord, Je - sus Christ, King of end - less glo - ry!

Verse: (Cantor)

to Refrain

God so loved   the world that he   gave   his   on - ly   Son, / ˙so that}
{everyone who believes in   him might   have   e - ter - nal   life.

RCIA Option: Third Sunday of Lent

March 3

(M.M. ♩ = c. 100)

Psalm 95:1-2, 6-7, 8-9

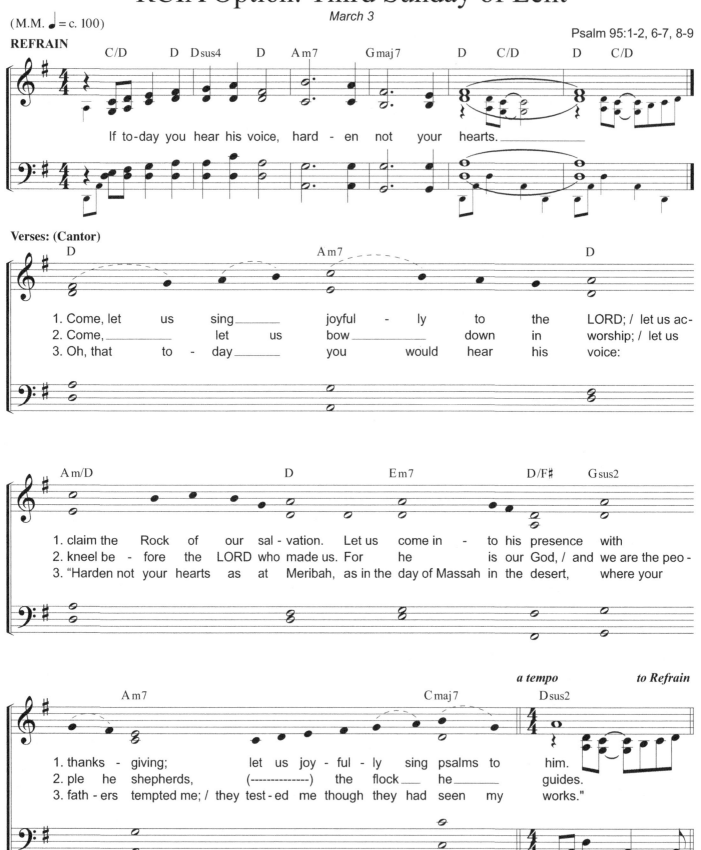

Gospel Acclamation: cf. John 4:42, 15

Acclamation: (Keyboard/SATB) NO. VI

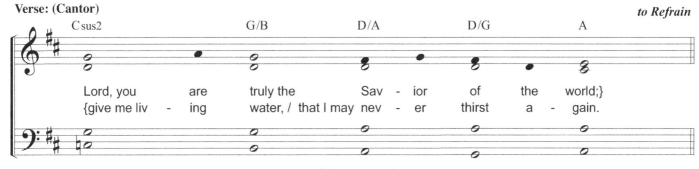

Praise to you, Lord Je - sus Christ, King of end - less glo - ry!

Verse: (Cantor)
to Refrain

Lord, you are truly the Sav - ior of the world;}
{give me liv - ing water, / that I may nev - er thirst a - gain.

Fourth Sunday of Lent

March 10

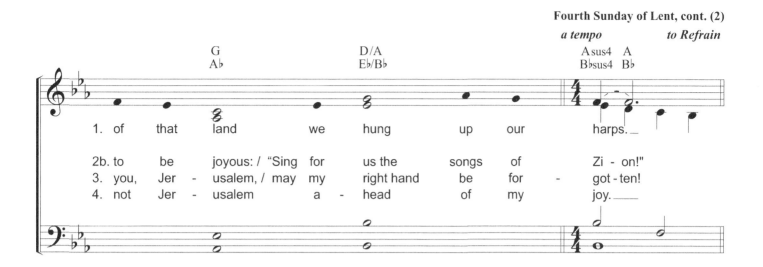

1. of that land we hung up our harps. _
2b. to be joyous: / "Sing for us the songs of Zi - on!"
3. you, Jer - usalem, / may my right hand be for - got - ten!
4. not Jer - usalem a - head of my joy. ___

Gospel Acclamation: John 3:16

Acclamation: (Keyboard/SATB) NO. VII

($\quad$ = c. 90)

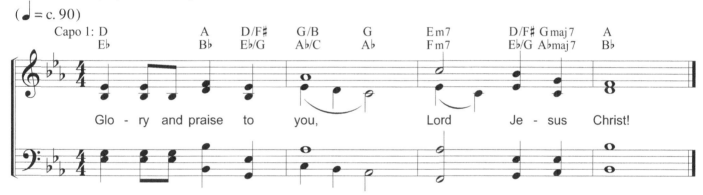

Glo - ry and praise to you, Lord Je - sus Christ!

Verse: (Cantor) *to Refrain*

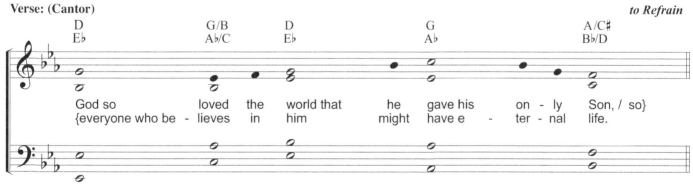

God so loved the world that he gave his on - ly Son, / so}
{everyone who be - lieves in him might have e - ter - nal life.

RCIA Option: Fourth Sunday of Lent

March 10

Gospel Acclamation: John 8:12

Acclamation: (Keyboard/SATB) NO. VI

(M.M. ♩ = c. 104)

Praise to you, Lord Je - sus Christ, King of end - less glo - ry!

Verse: (Cantor)

to Refrain

I am the light of the world, says the Lord; / whoever follows me will have the light of life.

Music © 2014, Timothy R. Smith. Published by TR TUNE, LLC. All rights reserved.

Fifth Sunday of Lent

March 17

Psalm 51:3–4, 12–13, 14–15

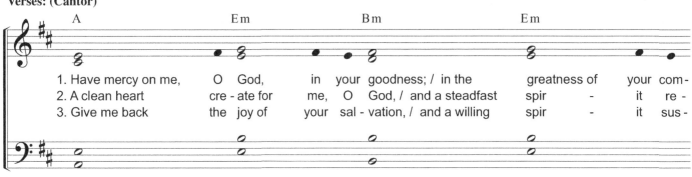

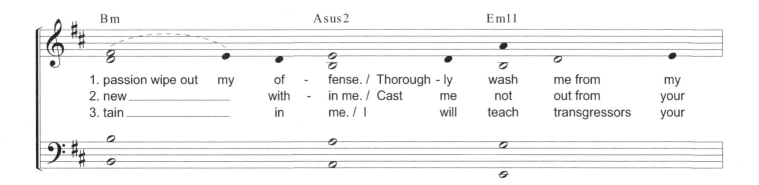

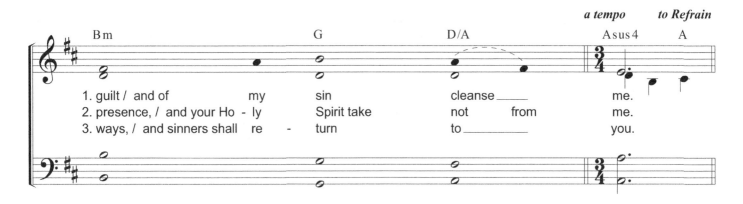

Gospel Acclamation: John 12:26

Acclamation: (Keyboard/SATB) NO. VI

(M.M. ♩ = c. 104)

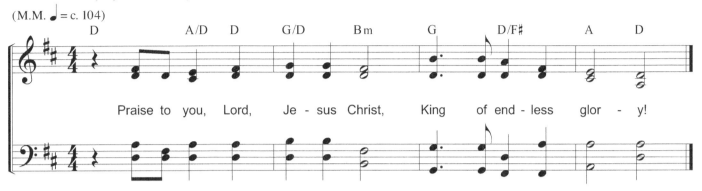

Praise to you, Lord, Je - sus Christ, King of end - less glor - y!

Verse: (Cantor)

to Refrain

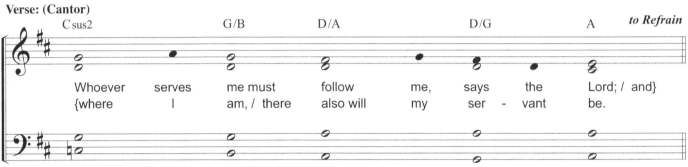

Whoever serves me must follow me, says the Lord; / and}
{where I am, / there also will my ser - vant be.

RCIA Option: Fifth Sunday of Lent

March 17

(M.M. ♩ = c. 80)

Psalm 130:1-2, 3-4, 5-6, 7-8

REFRAIN

Verses: (Cantor)

a tempo *to Refrain*

Gospel Acclamation: John 11:25a, 26

Acclamation: (Keyboard/SATB) NO. VI

(M.M. ♩ = c. 104)

Praise to you, Lord Je - sus Christ, King of end - less glo - ry!

Verse: (Cantor)   *to Refrain*

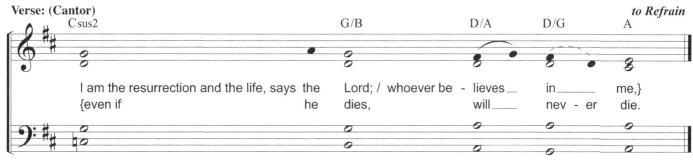

I am the resurrection and the life, says the Lord; / whoever be - lieves __ in _____ me,}
{even if   he dies,   will ____ nev - er die.

Palm Sunday of the Passion of the Lord

March 24

Psalm 22:8-9, 17-18, 19-20, 23-24

4. midst of the as-sembly I will praise you: "You who fear the LORD, praise him; all you des-

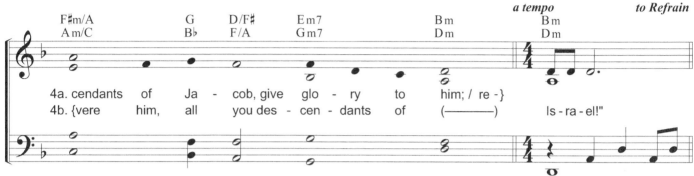

a tempo   *to Refrain*

4a. cendants of Ja - cob, give glo - ry to him; / re -}
4b. {vere him, all you des - cen - dants of (———) Is - ra - el!"

Gospel Acclamation: Philippians 2:8-9
Acclamation: (Keyboard/SATB) NO. VII

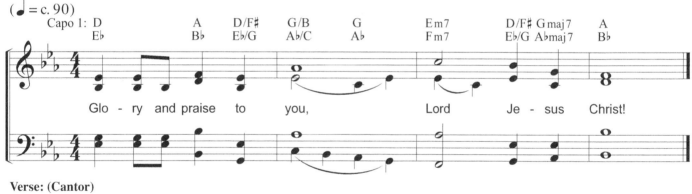

(♩ = c. 90)

Glo - ry and praise to you, Lord Je - sus Christ!

Verse: (Cantor)

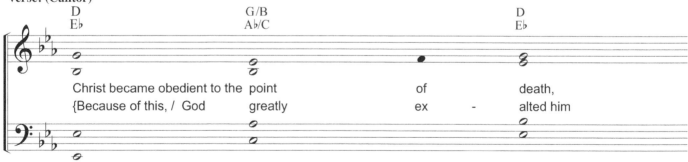

Christ became obedient to the point   of   death,
{Because of this, / God   greatly   ex - alted him

to Refrain

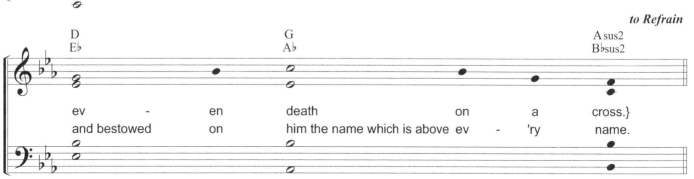

ev - en death   on   a   cross.}
and bestowed   on   him the name which is above ev - 'ry   name.

Thursday of the Lord's Supper (Holy Thursday):
At the Evening Mass

March 28

Psalm 116:12-13,15-16bc, 17-18

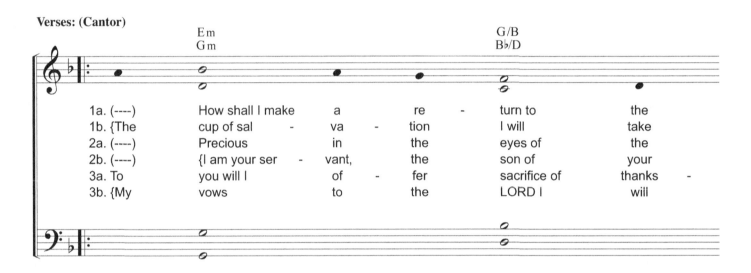

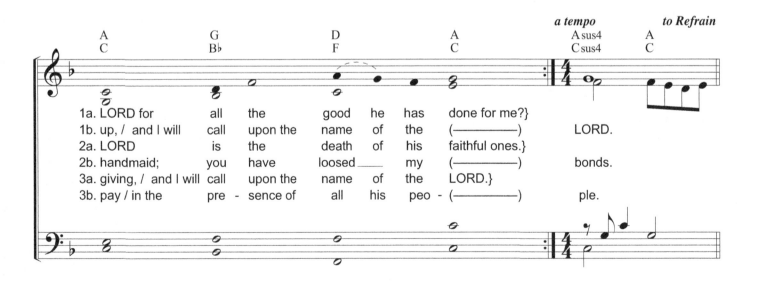

Gospel Acclamation: John 13:34

Acclamation: (Keyboard/SATB) NO. VII

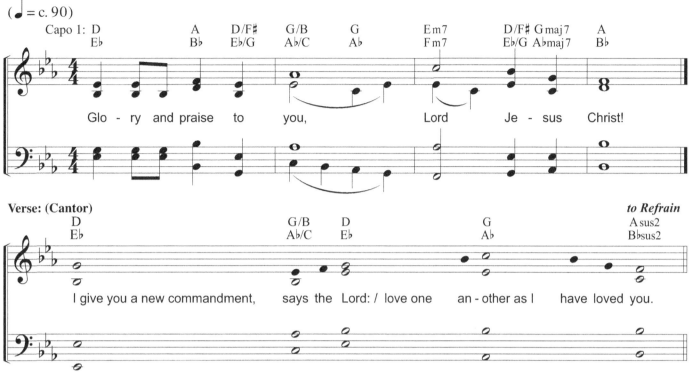

Friday of the Passion of the Lord (Good Friday)

March 29

(M.M. ♩ = c. 120)

Psalm 31:2, 6, 12-13, 15-16, 17, 25

Gospel Acclamation: Philippians 2:8-9

Acclamation: (Keyboard/SATB) NO. VII

Glo - ry and praise to you, Lord Je - sus Christ!

Verse: (Cantor)

Christ became obedient to the point of death,
{Because of this, / God greatly ex - alted him

to Refrain

ev - en death on a cross.}
and bestowed on him the name which is above every oth - er name.

The Easter Vigil in the Holy Night

Responsorial Psalm (following first reading) *March 30*

Psalm 104:1-2, 5-6, 10, 12, 13-14, 24, 35

Alternate Responsorial Psalm (Following first reading)

(M.M. ♩ = c. 61)

Psalm 33:4-5, 6-7, 12-13, 20 & 22

REFRAIN

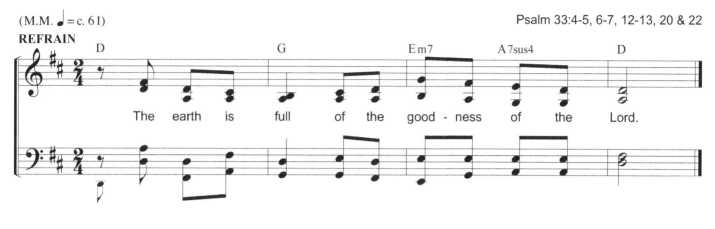

The earth is full of the good-ness of the Lord.

Verses: (Cantor)

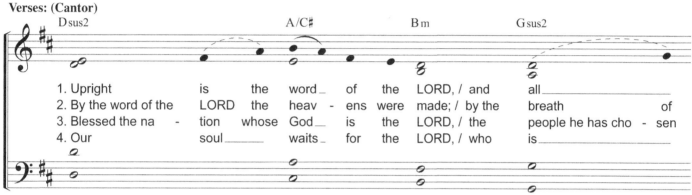

1. Upright is the word of the LORD, / and all
2. By the word of the LORD the heav-ens were made; / by the breath of
3. Blessed the na-tion whose God is the LORD, / the people he has cho-sen
4. Our soul waits for the LORD, / who is

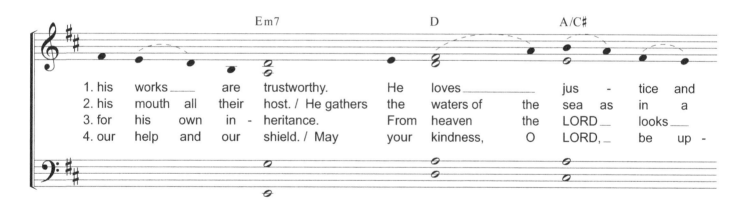

1. his works are trustworthy. He loves jus-tice and
2. his mouth all their host. / He gathers the waters of the sea as in a
3. for his own in-heritance. From heaven the LORD looks
4. our help and our shield. / May your kindness, O LORD, be up-

a tempo   *to Refrain*

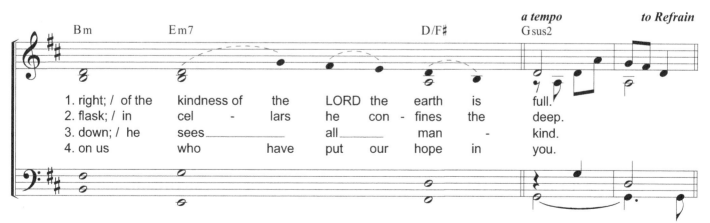

1. right; / of the kindness of the LORD the earth is full.
2. flask; / in cel-lars he con-fines the deep.
3. down; / he sees all man-kind.
4. on us who have put our hope in you.

Responsorial Psalm (following second reading)

(M.M. ♩ = c. 106)

Psalm 16:5, 8, 9-10,11

1. fore me;   with   him at my   right hand I   shall not be dis - turbed.
2. netherworld, nor will you suffer your faithful one to undergo   cor - rup -tion.
3. ever, / [for – (---)   ev-er.]

The Easter Vigil in the Holy Night, cont.
Responsorial Psalm (following third reading)

(M.M. ♩ = c. 102)

Exodus 15:1-2, 3-4, 5-6, 17-18

REFRAIN

Let us sing to the Lord; he has cov-ered him-self in glo - ry.

Verse 1: (Cantor)

1. I will sing to the LORD, for he is glori - ous-ly tri - umphant; horse and chariot he has

1a. cast in - to the sea. My strength and my cour-age is _____ the
1b.   {my God, _____ I

1a. LORD,   and   he has   been   my   sav - ior. / He is}
1b. praise him; / the God of my father,   I   ex - tol him.

a tempo   *to Refrain*

Verses 2 & 3: (Cantor)

2. The LORD is a war - rior,   LORD   is _____ his name!
3. The flood waters cov - ered them, / they sank into the depths like a stone.

2. Pharoah's chariots and army he hurled in - to the sea; / the e -
3. Your right hand, O LORD, mag-nifi - cent in power, your

2. lite of his officers were sub - merged in the Red___ Sea.
3. right hand, O LORD, has shat - tered the enemy.

Verse 4: (Cantor)

4. You brought in the people you re - deemed / and planted them on the mountain of your in -

4a. heritance — the place where you made your seat,___ O LORD,}
4b. {the sanctuary, LORD, which your hands___ es - tablished. The

4b. LORD___ shall reign for - ev - er and ever.

The Easter Vigil in the Holy Night, cont.
Responsorial Psalm (following fourth reading)

(M.M. ♩ = c. 118)
REFRAIN

Psalm 30:2, 4, 5-6, 11-12, 13

Verses: (Cantor)

1. I will ex-tol you, O LORD, for you drew me clear and did
2. Sing praise to the LORD, / you his faith-ful ones, / and give
3. Hear, O LORD, and have pity, [have pity] on me; / O, (—)

1. not let my enemies re-joice ov-er me. O
2. thanks to his ho-ly name. For his
3. (----------------------) LORD, be my helper. You

1. LORD, you brought me up from the neth-er-world; / you pre-
2. anger lasts but a moment; / a lifetime, his good will. / At
3. changed my mourning in-to dancing; / O LORD, my God, / for -

1. served me from a-mong those going down in-to the pit.
2. nightfall, weeping en-ters in, / but with the dawn, re-joicing.
3. ev-er will I give you thanks.

Responsorial Psalm (following fifth reading)

(M.M. ♩ = c. 120)

Isaiah 12:2-3, 4, 5-6

REFRAIN

Verses: (Cantor)

1a. God in - deed is my savior; / I am confident and un - a - fraid.}
1b. {My strength and my courage is the LORD, and he has been my savior.
2a. Give thanks to the LORD, ac - claim his name;}
2b. {a - mong the nations make known his deeds,
3a. Sing praise to the LORD for his glorious a - chievement;}
3b. {let this be known through - out all the earth.}
3c. {Shout with ex - ul - tation, O city of Zion,

a tempo to Refrain

1b. With joy you will draw wa - ter at the fountain of sal - vation.

2b. pro - claim how ex - alt - ed is his name.

3c. for great in your midst is the Holy One of Israel!

The Easter Vigil in the Holy Night, cont.

Responsorial Psalm (following sixth reading)

(M.M. ♩ = c. 124)

Psalm 19:8, 9, 10, 11

REFRAIN

Lord, you___ have the words,___ Lord, you___ have the words,___ you have the words of ev - er - last - ing life. *(Keyboard)*

Verses: (Cantor)

1. The law of the LORD is per - fect, / re - freshing the soul; / the de - cree of
2. The precepts of the LORD are right, re - joicing the heart; / the com -mand of
3. The fear of the LORD is pure, en - during for - ever; / the ordinances of
4. (---) They are more pre - cious than gold, than a heap of purest gold; sweeter

a tempo   *to Refrain*

1. the LORD is trust - worthy, / giving wisdom to the sim -ple.
2. the LORD is clear, en - lighten - ing the eye.
3. the LORD are true, (--------) all of them just.
4. al - so than syr - up / or honey from the comb.___

Option A, when Baptism is celebrated
Responsorial Psalm (following seventh reading)

(M.M. ♩ = c. 64)

Psalm 42:3, 5; 43:3, 4

REFRAIN

Like a deer that longs for run - ning streams, my soul___ longs for you, my

God, my soul___ longs for you, my God.

Verses: (Cantor)

1. Athirst is my soul for God, the liv - ing God.
2. I went with the throng and led them in pro - cession
3. Send forth your light and your fi - del - ity; they shall lead me on / and
4. Then will I go in to the altar of God, / the God of my glad - ness and joy;

to Refrain

1. When shall I go___ and be - hold the face___ of God?
2a. to the house___ of___ God, / a -}
2b. {mid loud cries of joy___ and thanks - giving, / with the multitude keep - ing festival.
3. bring me to your ho - ly___ mountain, / to your dwell - ing - place.
4. then will I give you thanks up - on the harp, O God,___ my God!

Or: Option B, when Baptism is not celebrated
Responsorial Psalm (following seventh reading)

Isaiah 12:2-3, 4bcd, 5-6

Or: Option C, when Baptism is not celebrated
Responsorial Psalm (following seventh reading)

Psalm 51:12-13, 14-15, 18-19

(M.M. ♩ = c. 77)

REFRAIN

Cre - ate ___ a clean heart, a clean heart in me, O God.

Verses: (Cantor)

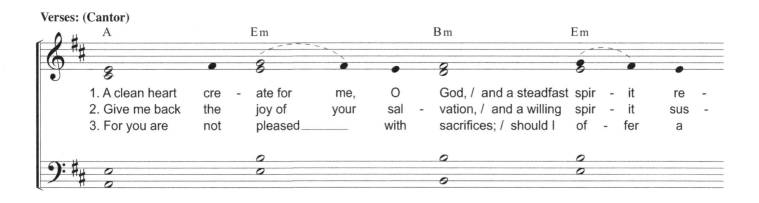

1. A clean heart cre - ate for me, O God, / and a steadfast spir - it re -
2. Give me back the joy of your sal - vation, / and a willing spir - it sus -
3. For you are not pleased ___ with sacrifices; / should I of - fer a

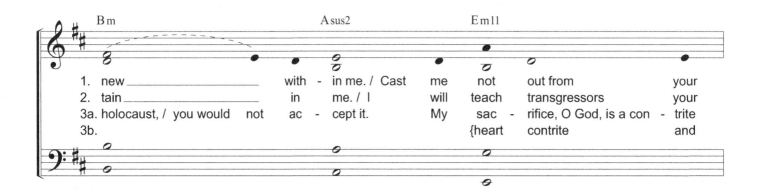

1. new ___ with - in me. / Cast me not out from your
2. tain ___ in me. / I will teach transgressors your
3a. holocaust, / you would not ac - cept it. My sac - rifice, O God, is a con - trite
3b. {heart contrite and

1. presence, / and your Ho - ly Spirit take not from me.
2. ways, / and sinners shall re - turn to ___ you.
3a. spirit; / a}
3b. humbled, O God, you will not spurn.

Responsorial Psalm: Psalm 118:1-2, 16-17, 22-23

Acclamation: (Keyboard/SATB) NO. II

(M.M. ♩ = c. 154)

Capo 3: A   G   D/F♯   E   E/D   A/C♯   D   D/F♯ Esus4   E
C   B♭   F/A   G   G/F   C/E   F   F/A   Gsus4   G

Al - le - lu - ia, al - le - lu - ia, al - le - lu - ia.

Verses: (Cantor)

A   Asus4
C   Csus4

1. Give thanks to the LORD, for he is
2. "The right hand of the LORD has struck with
3. The stone which the builders re - ject - ed

A   Asus4   A   E   A
C   Csus4   C   G   C

1. good, for his mer - cy en - dures for - ev - er. / Let the house of
2. power; the right hand of the LORD is ex - al - ted. / I shall not die, but
3. has be - come the cor - ner - stone. By the LORD has

Asus4   A   D/F♯   D   Bm/A A   *to Refrain*
Csus4   C   F/A   F   Dm/C C

1. Isra - el say, "His mer - cy en - dures for - ev - er."
2. live, and de - clare the works of the LORD."
3. this been done; / it is won - der - ful in our eyes.

Easter Sunday of the Resurrection of the Lord: At the Mass during the Day

March 31

(M.M. ♩ = c. 156)

REFRAIN [or: Alleluia]

Psalm 118:1-2, 16-17, 22-23

This is the day the Lord has made; let us re-joice and be glad.

Verses: (Cantor)

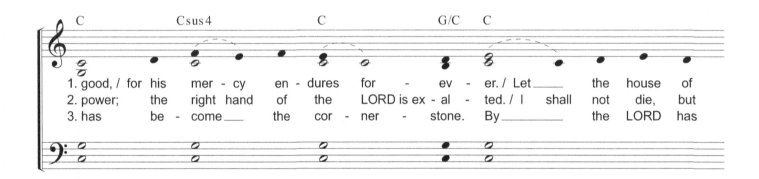

1. Give thanks to the LORD, for he is
2. "The right hand of the LORD has struck with
3. The stone which the builders re - ject - ed

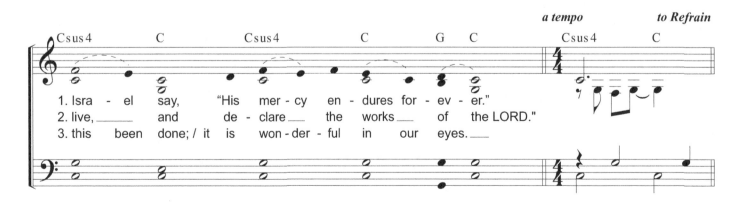

1. good, / for his mer-cy en-dures for - ev - er. / Let the house of
2. power; the right hand of the LORD is ex-al-ted. / I shall not die, but
3. has be-come the cor-ner-stone. By the LORD has

a tempo   *to Refrain*

1. Isra-el say, "His mer-cy en-dures for - ev - er."
2. live, and de-clare the works of the LORD."
3. this been done; / it is won-der-ful in our eyes.

84

Gospel Acclamation: cf. 1 Corinthians 5:7b-8a

Acclamation: (Keyboard/SATB) NO. V

Second Sunday of Easter (or Sunday of Divine Mercy)

(M.M. ♩ = c. 114)

April 7

Psalm 118:2-4, 13-15, 22-24

REFRAIN [or: Alleluia]

Give thanks to the Lord for he is good, his love is ev-er-last-ing.

Verse 1: (Cantor)

1. Let the house of Is-rael say, "His mer-cy en-dures for-ev-er." Let the house of Aar-on say, / "His mer-cy

a tempo *to Refrain*

1. en-dures for-ever." Let those who fear the LORD say, "His mer-cy en-dures forev-er."

Verse 2-3: (Cantor)

2. I was hard pressed and was fall-ing, but the LORD helped me.
3. The stone which the build-ers re-ject-ed has be-come the corner-stone.

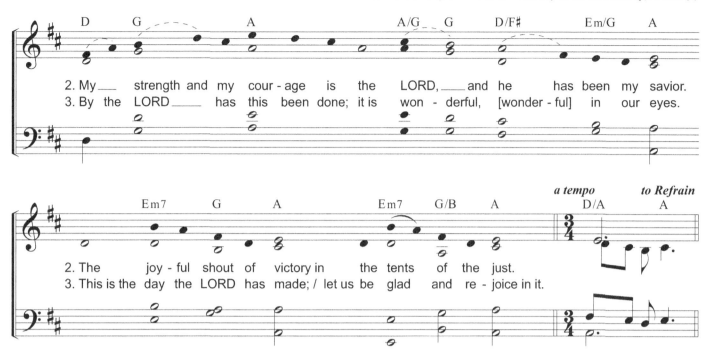

2. My __ strength and my cour-age is the LORD, __ and he has been my savior.
3. By the LORD __ has this been done; it is won - derful, [wonder - ful] in our eyes.

2. The joy - ful shout of victory in the tents of the just.
3. This is the day the LORD has made; / let us be glad and re - joice in it.

Gospel Acclamation: John 20:29
Acclamation: (Keyboard/SATB) NO. III
(M.M. ♩ = c. 160)

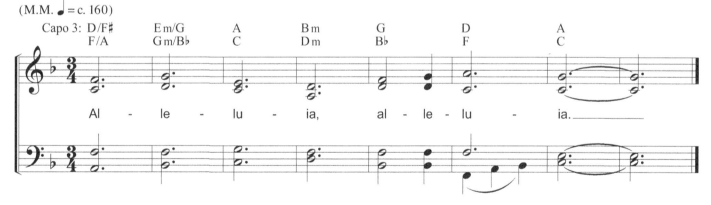

Al - le - lu - ia, al - le - lu - ia. ___

Verse: (Cantor)

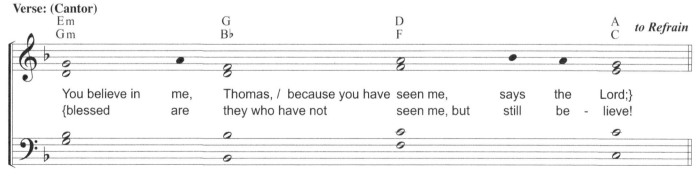

You believe in me, Thomas, / because you have seen me, says the Lord;}
{blessed are they who have not seen me, but still be - lieve!

Third Sunday of Easter

April 14

Psalm 4:2, 4, 7–8, 9

Gospel Acclamation: Luke 24:32

Acclamation: (Keyboard/SATB) NO. III

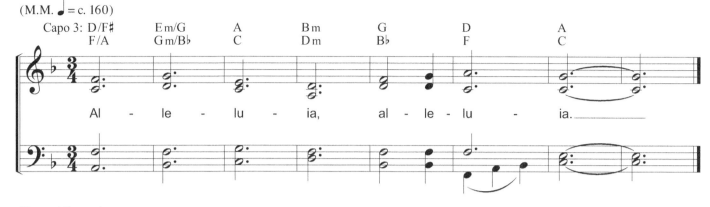

Al - le - lu - ia, al - le - lu - ia.___

Verse: (Cantor)

Lord___ Jesus, open the Scrip - tures to us;}
{make our hearts burn while you speak to us.

Fourth Sunday of Easter

April 21

1. ref - uge in the LORD than to trust in _____ princ-es. ____
2. LORD has this been done; it is wonderful in our eyes. ____
3. LORD, for he is good; for his kindness en-dures for - ev - er. ____

Gospel Acclamation: John 10:14

Acclamation: (Keyboard/SATB) NO. IV

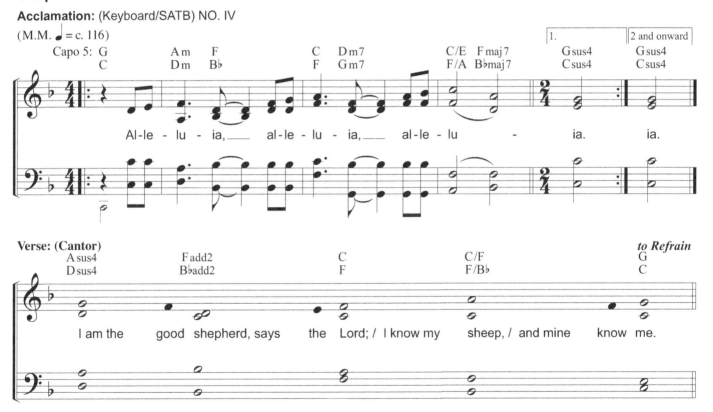

Al-le-lu - ia, ____ al-le-lu - ia, ____ al-le-lu - ia. ia.

Verse: (Cantor)

I am the good shepherd, says the Lord; / I know my sheep, / and mine know me.

Fifth Sunday of Easter

April 24

Gospel Acclamation: John 15:4a, 5b

Acclamation: (Keyboard/SATB) NO. IV

(M.M. ♩ = c. 116)

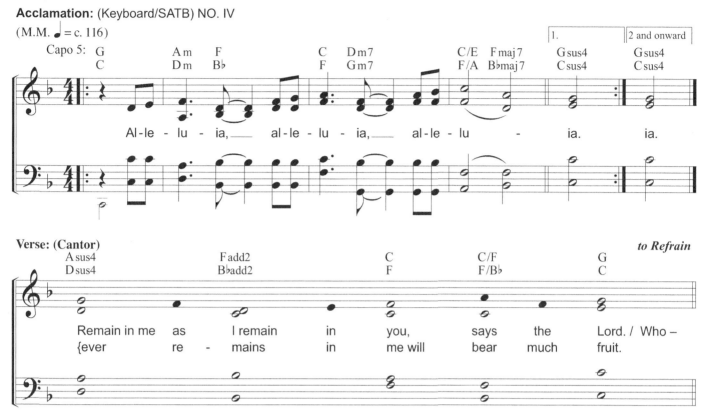

Al-le - lu - ia, ___ al-le - lu - ia, ___ al-le - lu - ia. ia.

Verse: (Cantor) *to Refrain*

Remain in me as I remain in you, says the Lord. / Who –
{ever re - mains in me will bear much fruit.

Sixth Sunday of Easter

May 5

Psalm 98:1, 2-3, 3-4

Gospel Acclamation: John 14:23

Acclamation: (Keyboard/SATB) NO. II

(M.M. ♩ = c. 130)

Al - le - lu - ia, al - le - lu - ia, al - le - lu - ia._____

Verse: (Cantor)

Whoever loves me will keep my word, says the Lord, / and my

Father will love him / and we will come to him.

Music © 2014, Timothy R. Smith. Published by TR TUNE, LLC. All rights reserved.

The Ascension of the Lord

May 9

The Ascension of the Lord may be celebrated on May 9 or transferred
to May 12, depending upon the practice of each province.

(M.M. ♩ = c. 138)

REFRAIN [or: Alleluia]

Psalm 47:2-3, 6-7, 8-9

Verses: (Cantor)

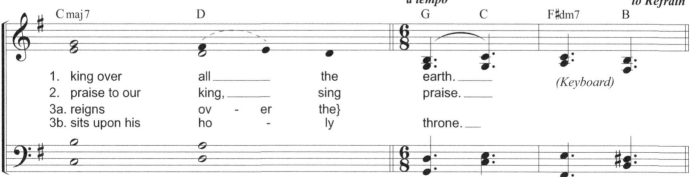

Gospel Acclamation: Matthew 28:19a, 20b

Acclamation: (Keyboard/SATB) NO. III

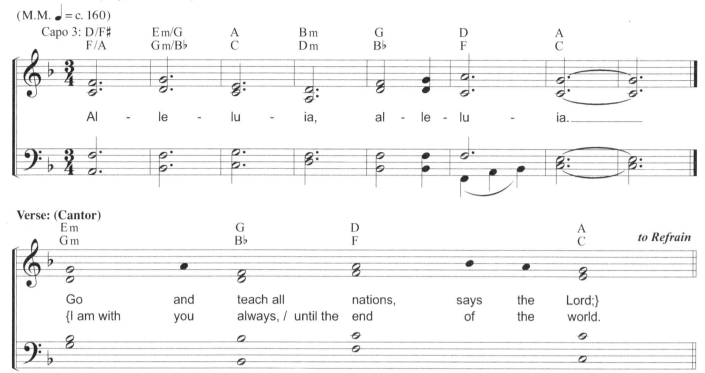

Verse: (Cantor)

Go   and   teach all   nations,   says   the   Lord;}
{I am with   you   always, / until the   end   of   the   world.

Seventh Sunday of Easter

May 12

(M.M. ♩ = c. 68)

Psalm 103:1–2, 11–12, 19–20

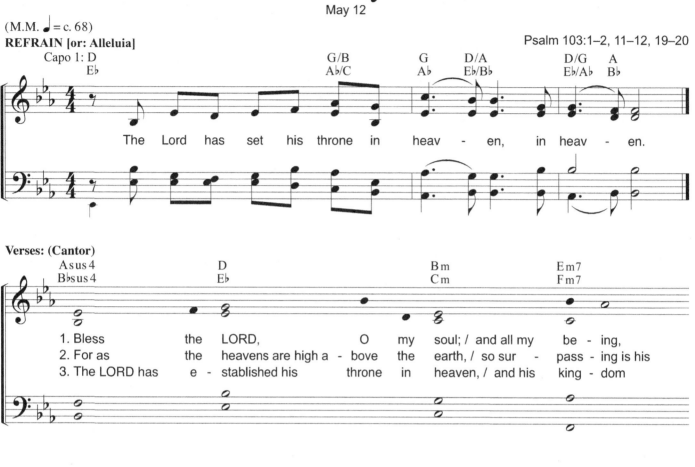

REFRAIN [or: Alleluia]

The Lord has set his throne in heav - en, in heav - en.

Verses: (Cantor)

1. Bless the LORD, O my soul; / and all my be - ing,
2. For as the heavens are high a - bove the earth, / so sur - pass - ing is his
3. The LORD has e - stablished his throne in heaven, / and his king - dom

1. bless his ho - ly name. Bless the LORD, O my
2. kindness toward those who fear him. As _____ far as the east is from the
3. rules ov - er all. Bless the LORD, all you his

a tempo   *to Refrain*

1. soul, / and for - get not all his be - ne - fits.
2. west, / so far has he put our trans - gressions from us. _____
3. angels, / you migh - ty in strength, who do his bid - ding. _____

Gospel Acclamation: cf. John 14:18

Acclamation: (Keyboard/SATB) NO. IV

Verse: (Cantor)

Pentecost Sunday: At the Vigil Mass
(Extended Form)
May 18

Psalm 33:10-11, 12-13, 14-15

Option 1:

Responsorial Psalm (following second reading)

(M.M. ♩ = c. 74)

Daniel 3:52, 53, 54, 55, 56

Verses 1-2: (Cantor)

Verses 3-5: (Cantor)

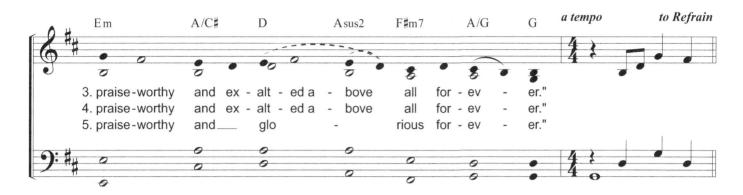

3. praise-worthy and ex - alt - ed a - bove all for - ev - er."
4. praise-worthy and ex - alt - ed a - bove all for - ev - er."
5. praise-worthy and____ glo - rious for - ev - er."

Pentecost Sunday: At the Vigil Mass (Extended Form), cont. (4)
Option 2:

Responsorial Psalm (following second reading)

(M.M. ♩ = c. 124)

Psalm 19:8, 9, 10, 11

REFRAIN

Verses: (Cantor)

Responsorial Psalm (following third reading)

(M.M. ♩ = c. 136)

REFRAIN [or: Alleluia]

Psalm 107:2-3, 4-5, 6-7, 8-9

Verses: (Cantor)

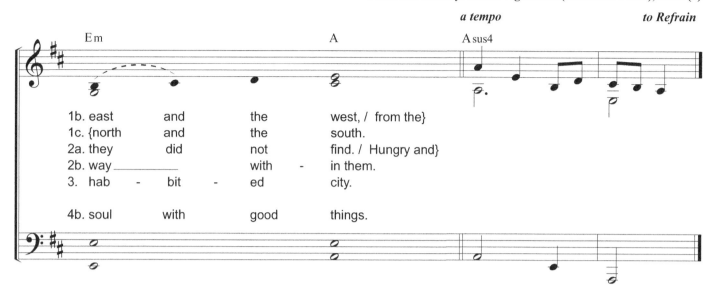

1b. east   and   the   west, / from the}
1c. {north   and   the   south.
2a. they   did   not   find. / Hungry and}
2b. way _____ with -   in them.
3. hab - bit - ed   city.

4b. soul   with   good   things.

Responsorial Psalm (following fourth reading)

(M.M. ♩ = c. 116)

Psalm 104:1-2, 24 & 35, 27-28, 29-30

REFRAIN [or: Alleluia]

Lord, send out your Spir - it, and re-new the face of the earth.

Verses: (Cantor)

1. Bless the LORD, O my soul! / O LORD, my God, you are
2. (---------------------) How man - i - fold are your works,

3. Crea - tures all look to you to give them
4. If you take a - way their breath, they perish / and re - turn

1. great in - deed! You are clothed with majesty and
2. O LORD! In wisdom you have wrought them

3. food in due time. When you give it to them, they
4. to their dust. When you send forth your

a tempo   **to Refrain**

1. glory, / robed in light as with a cloak.
2a. all – the earth is full of your creatures; / bless}
2b. {the LORD, O my soul!}
2c. {Al - le - lu - ia.
3. gather it; / when you open your hand, they are filled with good things.
4a. spir - it, they are cre - ated, / and you}
4b. {re - new the face of the earth.

Gospel Acclamation:

Acclamation: (Keyboard/SATB) NO. V

Al - le-lu - ia, al - le-lu - ia. Al - le-lu - ia, al - le-lu - ia.

Verse: (Cantor)

to Refrain

Come, Holy Spirit, fill the hearts of your faithful / and kin-dle in them the fire of your love.

Pentecost Sunday: At the Mass during the Day

May 19

Gospel Acclamation:

Acclamation: (Keyboard/SATB) NO. V

Verse: (Cantor)   *to Refrain*

The Most Holy Trinity

May 26

Gospel Acclamation: cf. Revelation 1:8

Acclamation: (Keyboard/SATB) NO. I

Verse: (Cantor)

to Refrain

Glory to the Father, the Son, and the Ho - ly Spirit; / to God who is, who was, / and who is to come.

The Most Holy Body and Blood of Christ
(Corpus Christi)

June 2

Psalm 116:12-13, 15-16, 17-18

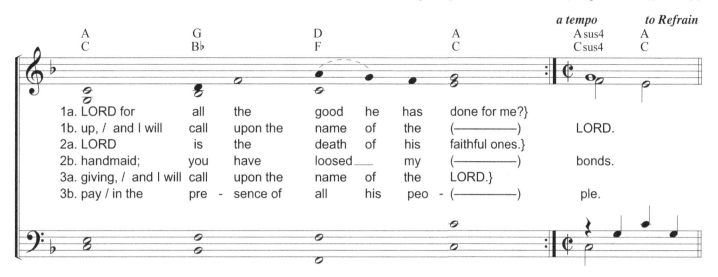

1a. LORD for all the good he has done for me?}
1b. up, / and I will call upon the name of the (————) LORD.
2a. LORD is the death of his faithful ones.}
2b. handmaid; you have loosed____ my (————) bonds.
3a. giving, / and I will call upon the name of the LORD.}
3b. pay / in the pre - sence of all his peo - (————) ple.

Gospel Acclamation: John 6:51

Acclamation: (Keyboard/SATB) NO. II

(M.M. ♩ = c. 130)

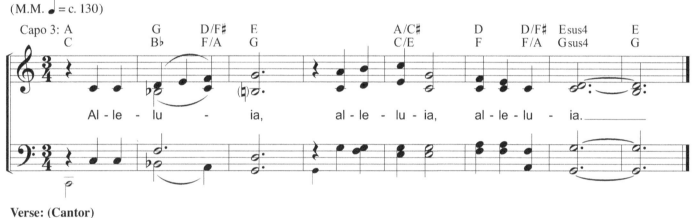

Al - le - lu - ia, al - le - lu - ia, al - le - lu - ia._____

Verse: (Cantor)

I am the living bread that came down from heaven, says the Lord; / whoever

eats this bread will live for - ever.

10th Sunday in Ordinary Time

June 9

Psalm 130:1-2, 3-4, 5-6, 7-8

(M.M. ♩ = c. 80)

REFRAIN

With the Lord there is mer-cy and full-ness of _____ re-demp-tion. *(Keyboard)*

Verses: (Cantor)

1. Out of the depths I cry to you, O LORD;
2. If _____ you, O LORD, _____ mark in - iquities,
3. I trust _____ in the LORD; _____ my _____ soul
4. For with the LORD is kind - ness and with him is

1. LORD, hear my voice! Let your ears be at -
2. LORD, who can stand? But with you is for -
3. trusts in his word. More than sen - tin - els
4. plente - ous re - demption; (--) and he will re -

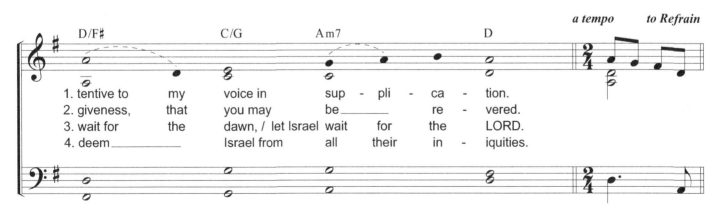

a tempo   *to Refrain*

1. tentive to my voice in sup - pli - ca - tion.
2. giveness, that you may be _____ re - vered.
3. wait for the dawn, / let Israel wait for the LORD.
4. deem _____ Israel from all their in - iquities.

Through composed version in *With the Lord* songbook Ed. 92562 available at www.ocp.org.

Gospel Acclamation: John 12:31b–32

Acclamation: (Keyboard/SATB) NO. I

Verse: (Cantor)   *to Refrain*

Now the ruler   of   this   world will be driv - en   out,   says   the   Lord; / and}
{when I am lifted up   from   the   earth, / I will   draw everyone   to   my - self.

11th Sunday in Ordinary Time

June 16

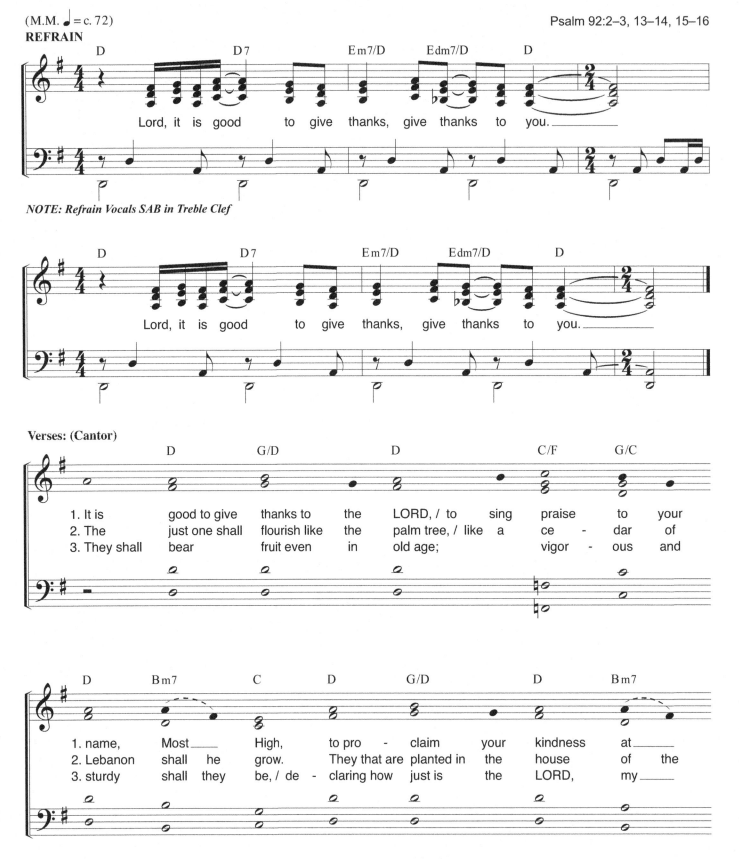

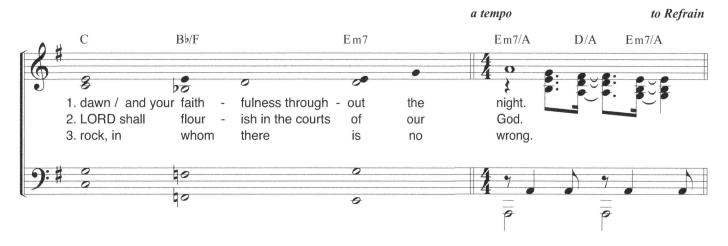

1. dawn / and your faith - fulness through - out the night.
2. LORD shall flour - ish in the courts of our God.
3. rock, in whom there is no wrong.

Gospel Acclamation:

Acclamation: (Keyboard/SATB) NO. IV

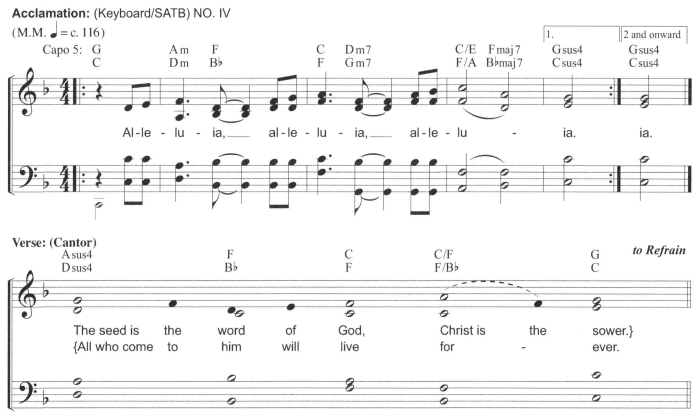

Al-le - lu - ia,___ al-le-lu - ia,___ al-le-lu - ia. ia.

Verse: (Cantor)

The seed is the word of God, Christ is the sower.}
{All who come to him will live for - ever.

12th Sunday in Ordinary Time

June 23

Psalm 107:23-24, 25-26, 28-29, 30-31

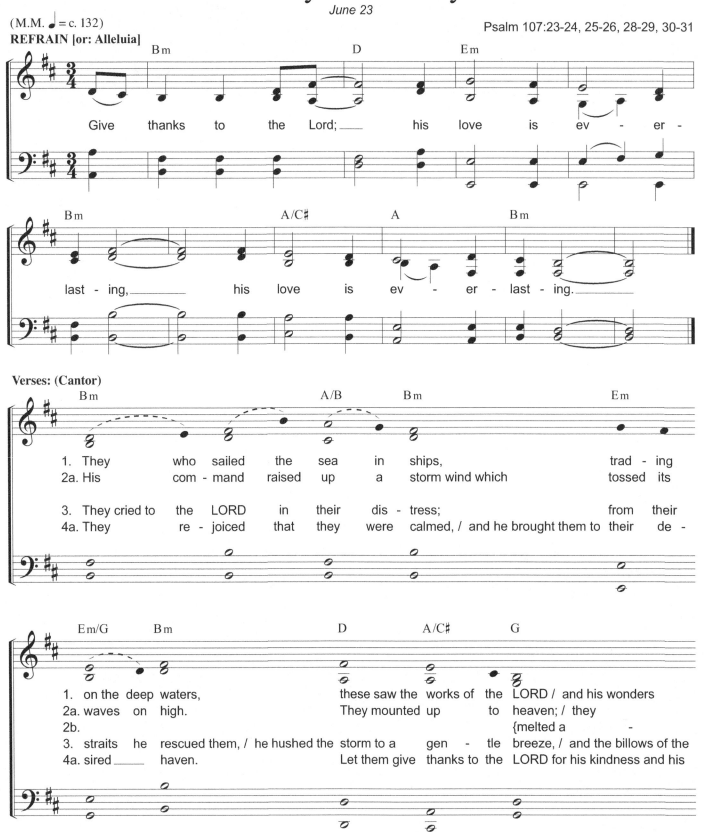

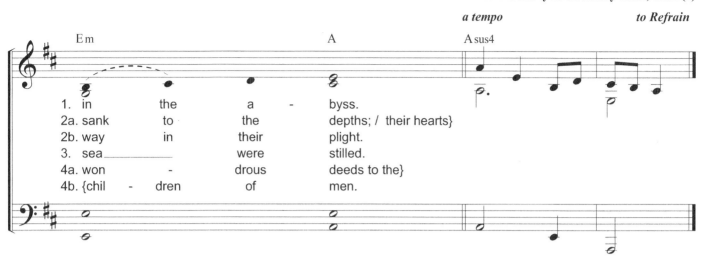

1. in the a - byss.
2a. sank to the depths; / their hearts}
2b. way in their plight.
3. sea_____ were stilled.
4a. won - drous deeds to the}
4b. {chil - dren of men.

Gospel Acclamation: Luke 7:16

Acclamation: (Keyboard/SATB) NO. IV

Al - le - lu - ia,____ al - le - lu - ia,____ al - le - lu - ia. ia.

Verse: (Cantor)

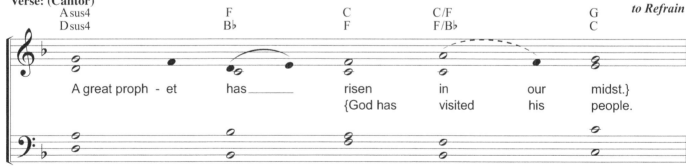

A great proph - et has____ risen in our midst.}
{God has visited his people.

13th Sunday in Ordinary Time

June 30

Psalm 30:2, 4, 5-6, 11-12, 13

Gospel Acclamation: cf. 2 Timothy 1:10

Acclamation: (Keyboard/SATB) NO. IV

(M.M. ♩ = c. 116)

Verse: (Cantor)

Our Sav - ior Je - sus Christ de - stroyed____ death}
{and brought life to light through the Gospel.

to Refrain

Music © 2014, Timothy R. Smith. Published by TR TUNE, LLC. All rights reserved.

14th Sunday in Ordinary Time
July 7

(M.M. ♩ = c. 124)

Psalm 123:1–2, 2, 3–4

a tempo   *to Refrain*

1. hands of their mas - ters.
2. pit - y on us. _____
3b. tempt of the proud. _____

Gospel Acclamation: cf. Luke 4:18

Acclamation: (Keyboard/SATB) NO. IV

(M.M. ♩ = c. 116)

Al-le - lu - ia,_____ al-le - lu - ia,_____ al-le - lu - ia. ia.

Verse: (Cantor)   *to Refrain*

The Spirit of the LORD is up - on me / for he sent me to bring glad tidings to the poor.

15th Sunday in Ordinary Time
July 14

(M.M. ♩ = c. 90)

REFRAIN

Psalm 85:9-10, 11-12, 13-14

Lord, let us see your kind-ness, and grant us your sal - va - tion._____

Verses: (Cantor)

1. I will hear what God pro - claims; the_____ LORD — / for he pro - claims_____
2. Kindness and truth shall meet; / jus - tice and peace shall_____
3. The LORD himself will give his benefits; our_____ land shall yield its

1. peace. / Near in - deed is his sal - vation to
2. kiss. / Truth shall spring out of the earth, and
3. increase. (—) Justice shall walk be - fore him, / and pre -

a tempo   *to Refrain*

1. those who fear him, glory dwel - ling in our land.____
2. jus - tice shall look down____ from____ heav-en.
3. pare_____ the____ way____ of his steps.____

Gospel Acclamation: Ephesians 1:17-18

Acclamation: (Keyboard/SATB) NO. II

(M.M. ♩ = c. 130)

Verse: (Cantor)   *to Refrain*

Music © 2014, Timothy R. Smith. Published by TR TUNE, LLC. All rights reserved.

16th Sunday in Ordinary Time

July 21

Gospel Acclamation: John 10:27

Acclamation: (Keyboard/SATB) NO. IV

(M.M. ♩ = c. 116)

Al-le - lu - ia,___ al-le - lu - ia,___ al-le - lu - ia. ia.

Verse: (Cantor)

My sheep hear my voice, says the Lord; / I know them, and they follow me.

Music © 2014, Timothy R. Smith. Published by TR TUNE, LLC. All rights reserved.

17th Sunday in Ordinary Time

July 28

(M.M. ♩ = c. 84)

Psalm 145:10–11, 15–16, 17–18

REFRAIN

The hand of the Lord feeds us; he an-swers all our needs. *(Keyboard)*

Verses: (Cantor)

1. Let all your works give you thanks, O___ LORD, / and let your faith-
2. The eyes of all___ look hopeful-ly to you, / and you give them their
3. The LORD is just in all his ways and holy in

1. ful ones___ bless___ you. Let them dis-course of the glory of your
2. food in due sea-son; you o-pen your hand and___
3. all his___ works.___ The LORD is near___ to all who call up-

a tempo — *to Refrain*

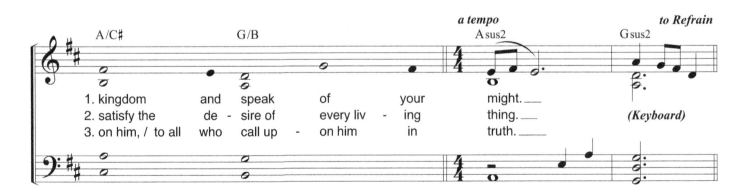

1. kingdom and speak of your might.___
2. satisfy the de-sire of every liv-ing thing.___ *(Keyboard)*
3. on him, / to all who call up-on him in truth.___

Gospel Acclamation: Luke 7:16

Acclamation: (Keyboard/SATB) NO. III

Al - le - lu - ia, al - le - lu - ia.

Verse: (Cantor)

A great prophet has risen in our midst. God has visited his people.

18th Sunday in Ordinary Time

August 4

(M.M. ♩ = c. 64)

Psalm 78:3–4, 23–24, 25, 54

REFRAIN

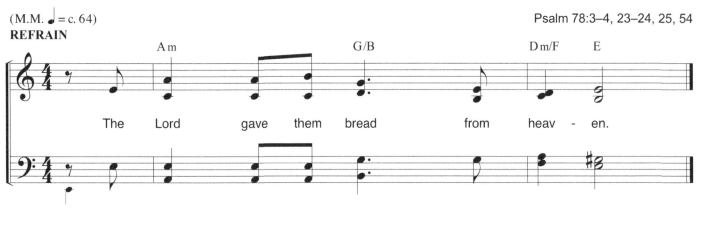

The Lord gave them bread from heav-en.

Verses: (Cantor)

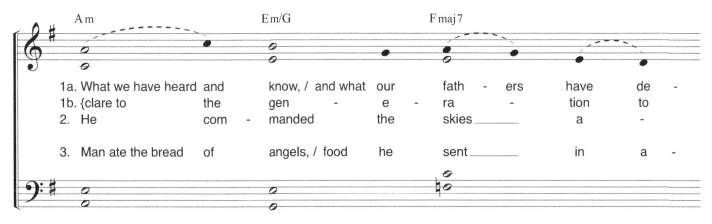

1a. What we have heard and know, / and what our fath-ers have de-
1b. {clare to the gen - e - ra - tion to
2. He com - manded the skies____ a -
3. Man ate the bread of angels, / food he sent____ in a -

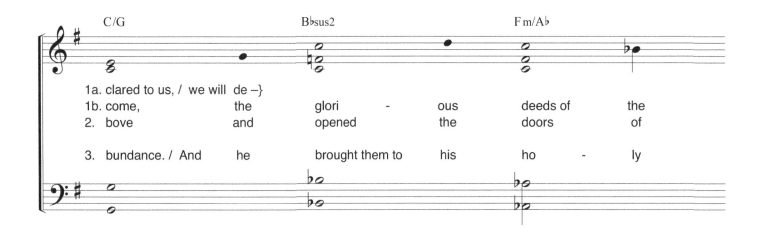

1a. clared to us, / we will de –}
1b. come, the glori - ous deeds of the
2. bove and opened the doors of
3. bundance. / And he brought them to his ho - ly

a tempo   to Refrain

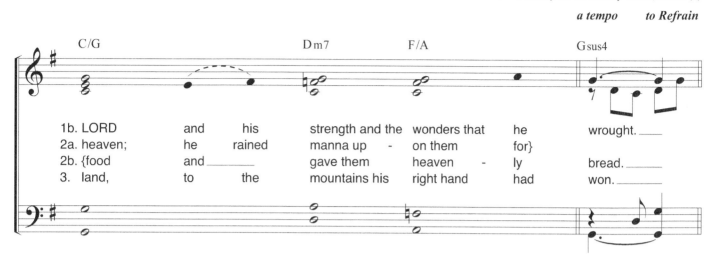

1b. LORD and his strength and the wonders that he wrought. ____
2a. heaven; he rained manna up - on them for}
2b. {food and ____ gave them heaven - ly bread. ____
3. land, to the mountains his right hand had won. ____

Gospel Acclamation: Matthew 4:4b

Acclamation: (Keyboard/SATB) NO. IV

(M.M. ♩ = c. 116)

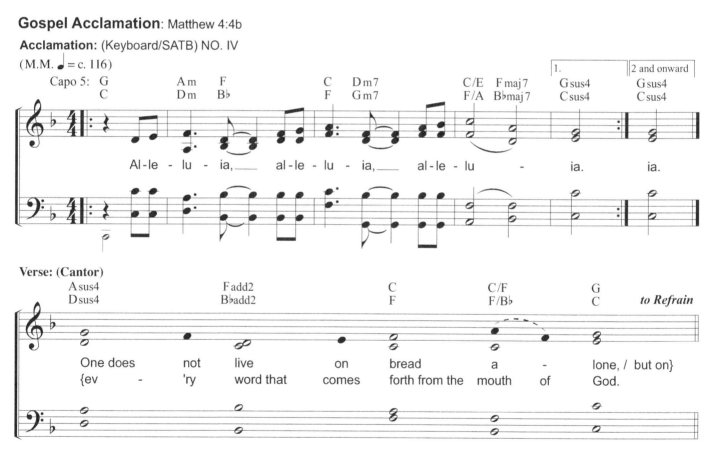

Al-le-lu - ia, ____ al-le-lu - ia, ____ al-le-lu - ia. ia.

Verse: (Cantor)

One does not live on bread a - lone, / but on}
{ev - 'ry word that comes forth from the mouth of God.

19th Sunday in Ordinary Time

August 11

Music: Timothy R. Smith
Psalm 34:2-3, 4-5, 6-7, 8-9

Verses: (Cantor)

1. I will bless the LORD at all times; / his praise shall be ever in my
2. Glor - i - fy the LORD with me, / let us to - geth - er ex - tol his
3. Look to him that you may be radiant with joy, / and your faces may not blush with
4. The an - gel of the LORD encamps around those who fear him and de -

1. mouth. Let my soul glory in the
2. name. / I sought the LORD, / and he an - swered
3. shame. / When the af - flicted man called out, / the LORD
4. livers them. Taste and see how good the LORD

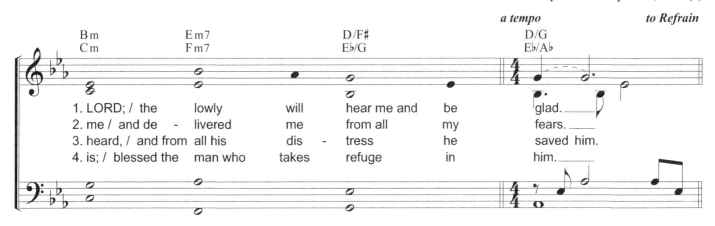

Gospel Acclamation: John 6:51

Acclamation: (Keyboard/SATB) NO. II

(M.M. ♩ = c. 130)

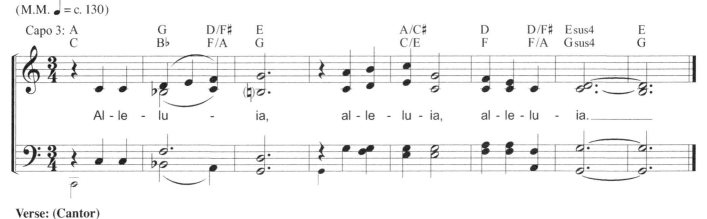

Verse: (Cantor)

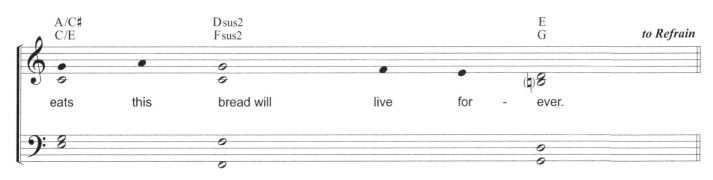

The Assumption of the Blessed Virgin Mary:
At the Vigil Mass

August 14

Psalm 132:6-7, 9-10, 13-14

Gospel Acclamation: Luke 11:28

Acclamation: (Keyboard/SATB) NO. III

(M.M. ♩ = c. 160)

Al - le - lu - ia, al - le - lu - ia.

Verse: (Cantor)

Blessed are they who hear the word of God and ob - serve it.

The Assumption of the Blessed Virgin Mary:
At the Mass during the Day

August 15

(M.M. ♩ = c. 68)

Psalm 45:10, 11, 12, 16

REFRAIN

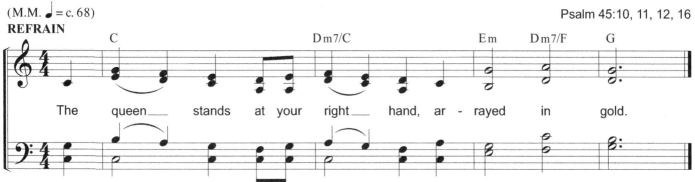

The queen stands at your right hand, ar-rayed in gold.

Verses: (Cantor)

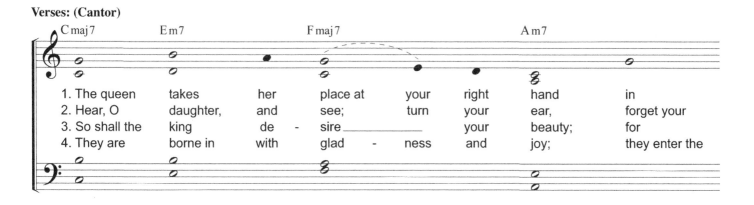

1. The queen takes her place at your right hand in
2. Hear, O daughter, and see; turn your ear, forget your
3. So shall the king de - sire your beauty; for
4. They are borne in with glad - ness and joy; they enter the

a tempo   *to Refrain*

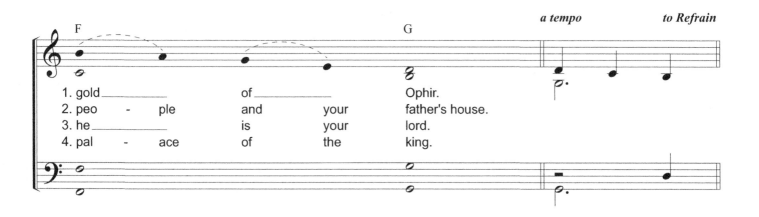

1. gold of Ophir.
2. peo - ple and your father's house.
3. he is your lord.
4. pal - ace of the king.

Gospel Acclamation:

Acclamation: (Keyboard/SATB) NO. III

(M.M. ♩ = c. 160)

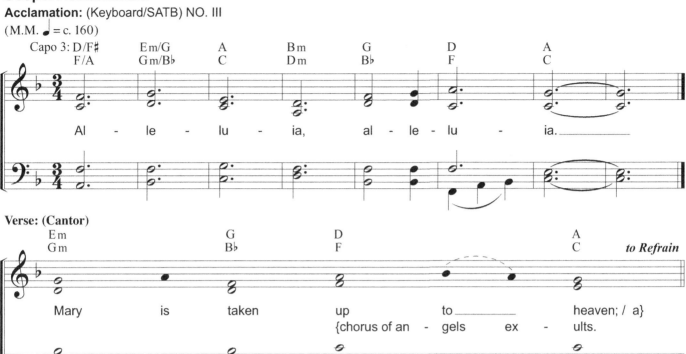

Verse: (Cantor)

Mary is taken up to _____ heaven; / a}
{chorus of an - gels ex - ults.

to Refrain

20th Sunday in Ordinary Time

August 18

Music: Timothy R. Smith
Psalm 34:2-3, 4-5, 6-7

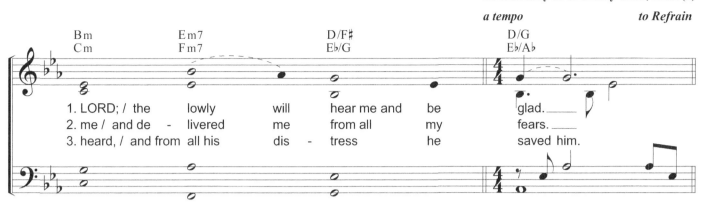

Gospel Acclamation: John 6:56

Acclamation: (Keyboard/SATB) NO. II

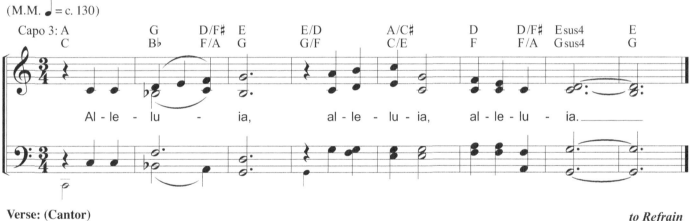

Verse: (Cantor)

21st Sunday in Ordinary Time

August 25

Music: Timothy R. Smith
Psalm 34:2–3, 16–17, 18–19, 20–21

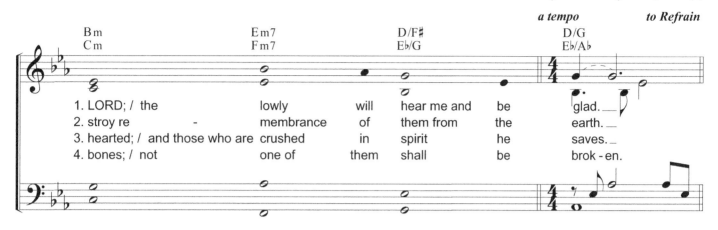

Gospel Acclamation: John 6:63c, 68c
Acclamation: (Keyboard/SATB) NO. III

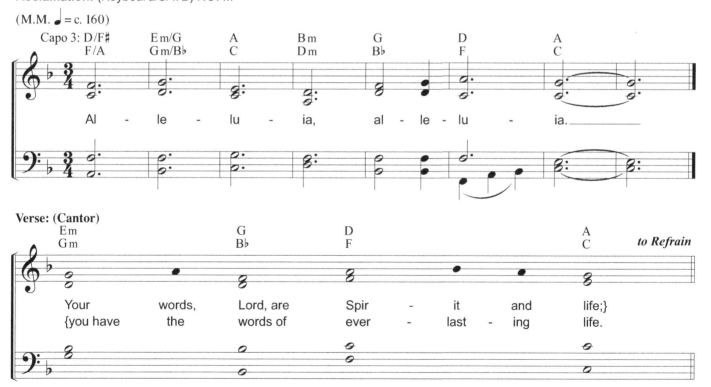

22nd Sunday in Ordinary Time

September 1

Gospel Acclamation: James 1:18

Acclamation: (Keyboard/SATB) NO. I

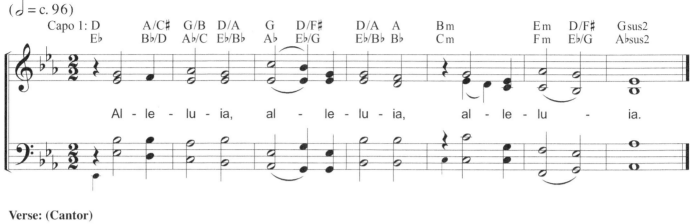

Al - le - lu - ia, al - le - lu - ia, al - le - lu - ia.

Verse: (Cantor)

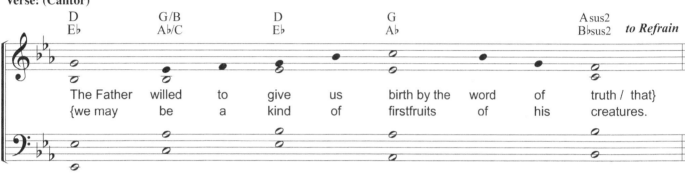

The Father willed to give us birth by the word of truth / that}
{we may be a kind of firstfruits of his creatures.

23rd Sunday in Ordinary Time

September 8

Gospel Acclamation: cf. Matthew 4:23

Acclamation: (Keyboard/SATB) NO. I

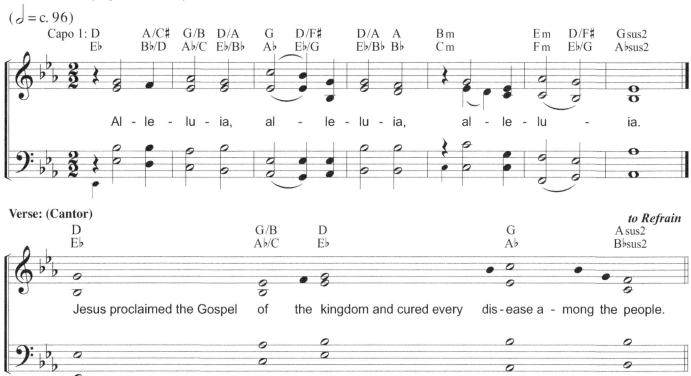

Al - le - lu - ia, al - le - lu - ia, al - le - lu - ia.

Verse: (Cantor)

to Refrain

Jesus proclaimed the Gospel of the kingdom and cured every dis-ease a - mong the people.

24th Sunday in Ordinary Time

September 15

(M.M. ♩ = c. 72)

Psalm 116:1–2, 3–4, 5–6, 8–9

REFRAIN [or: Alleluia]

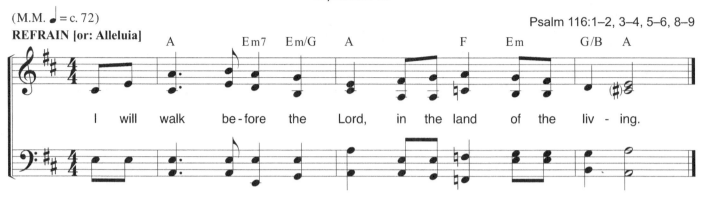

I will walk be-fore the Lord, in the land of the liv - ing.

Verses: (Cantor)

1. I love the LORD be - cause _____ he has heard my
2. The cords of death en - com - passed me; / the snares of the
3. (_____) Gracious is the LORD _____ and _____ just; / yes, our
4. For he has freed my soul from death, my

1. voice in sup - pli - ca - tion, / because (_____)
2. netherworld seized up - on me; / I fell into dis - tress and sorrow, / and I
3. God is _____ mer - ciful. / The LORD keeps the little ones;
4. eyes from _____ tears, my feet from _____ stumbling. / I shall

a tempo   **to Refrain**

1. he has inclined his ear to me the day I called. _____
2. called upon the name of the LORD, / "O LORD, save my life. _____
3. I was brought low, / and he _____ saved me.
4. walk before the LORD in the land of the liv - ing.

Gospel Acclamation: Galatians 6:14

Acclamation: (Keyboard/SATB) NO. II

(M.M. ♩ = c. 130)

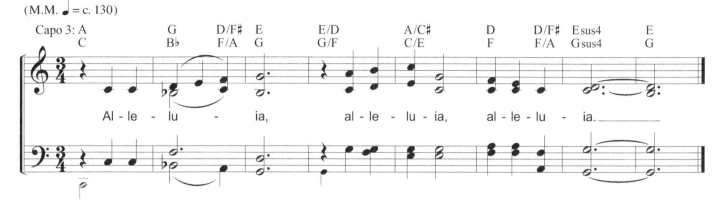

Al - le - lu - ia, al - le - lu - ia, al - le - lu - ia.____

Verse: (Cantor)   *to Refrain*

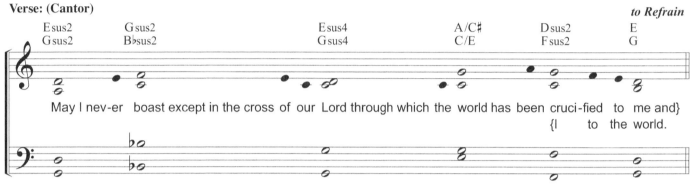

May I nev-er boast except in the cross of our Lord through which the world has been cruci-fied to me and}
{I to the world.

Music © 2014, Timothy R. Smith. Published by TR TUNE, LLC. All rights reserved.

25th Sunday in Ordinary Time

September 22

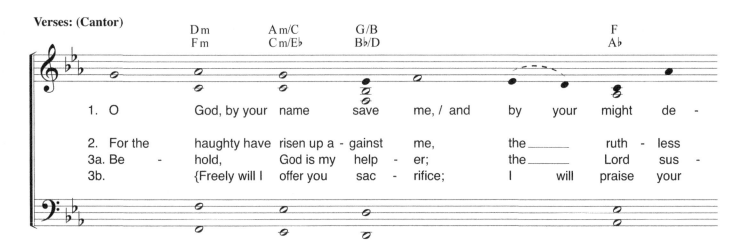

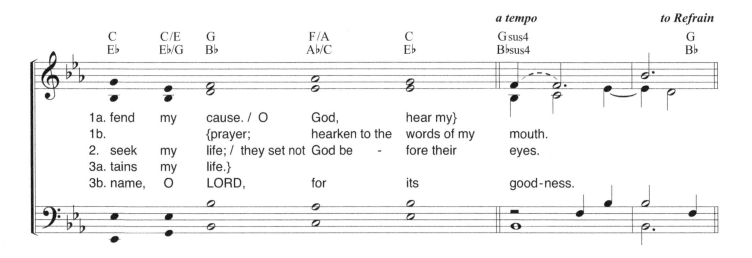

Gospel Acclamation: cf. 2 Thessalonians 2:14

Acclamation: (Keyboard/SATB) NO. IV

(M.M. ♩ = c. 116)

Capo 5: G / C — Am / Dm — F / B♭ — C / F — Dm7 / Gm7 — C/E / F/A — Fmaj7 / B♭maj7 — Gsus4 / Csus4 — Gsus4 / Csus4

1. | 2 and onward

Al-le-lu-ia,___ al-le-lu-ia,___ al-le-lu - ia. ia.

Verse: (Cantor)

to Refrain

Asus4 / Dsus4 — Fadd2 / B♭add2 — C / F — C/F / F/B♭ — G / C

God has called us through the Gospel / to pos-sess the glory of our Lord Je-sus Christ.

Music © 2014, Timothy R. Smith. Published by TR TUNE, LLC. All rights reserved.

26th Sunday in Ordinary Time

September 29

Psalm 19:8, 10, 12–13, 14

(M.M. ♩ = c. 74)

REFRAIN

The pre-cepts of the Lord give joy to the heart, joy to the heart.

Verses: (Cantor)

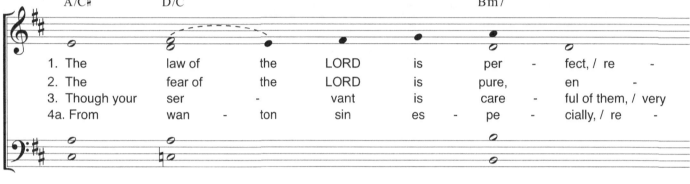

1. The law of the LORD is per - fect, / re -
2. The fear of the LORD is pure, en -
3. Though your ser - vant is care - ful of them, / very
4a. From wan - ton sin es - pe - cially, / re -

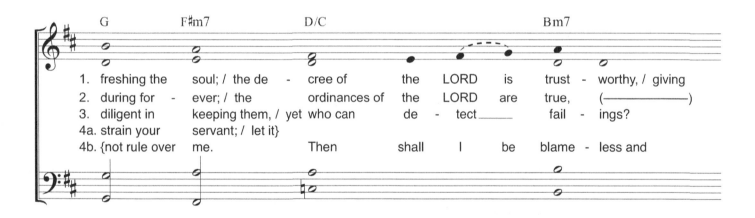

1. freshing the soul; / the de - cree of the LORD is trust - worthy, / giving
2. during for - ever; / the ordinances of the LORD are true, (———)
3. diligent in keeping them, / yet who can de - tect___ fail - ings?
4a. strain your servant; / let it}
4b. {not rule over me. Then shall I be blame - less and

a tempo *to Refrain*

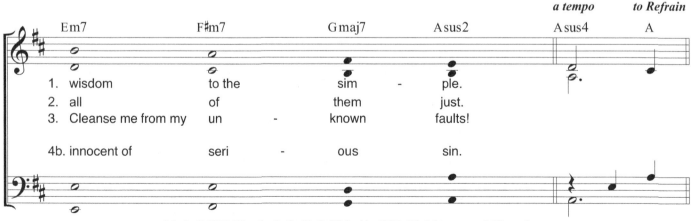

1. wisdom to the sim - ple.
2. all of them just.
3. Cleanse me from my un - known faults!

4b. innocent of seri - ous sin.

Gospel Acclamation: cf. John 17:17b, 17a

Acclamation: (Keyboard/SATB) NO. I

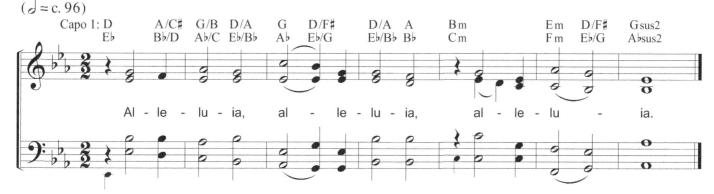

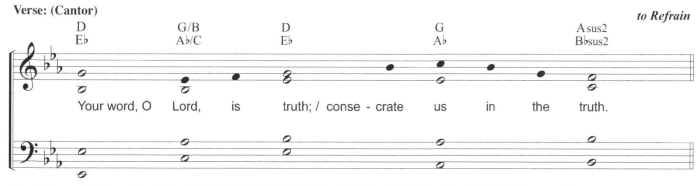

Music: Mass of the Sacred Heart; Timothy R. Smith © 2007, 2010, Timothy R. Smith. Published by OCP. All rights reserved.

27th Sunday in Ordinary Time

October 6

Psalm 128:1-2, 3, 4-5, 6

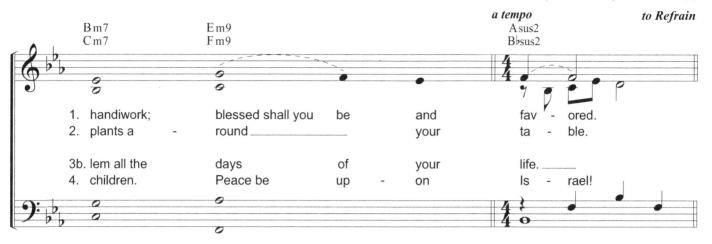

1. handiwork; blessed shall you be and fav - ored.
2. plants a - round _____ your ta - ble.

3b. lem all the days of your life. _____
4. children. Peace be up - on Is - rael!

Gospel Acclamation: 1 John 4:12
Acclamation: (Keyboard/SATB) NO. I

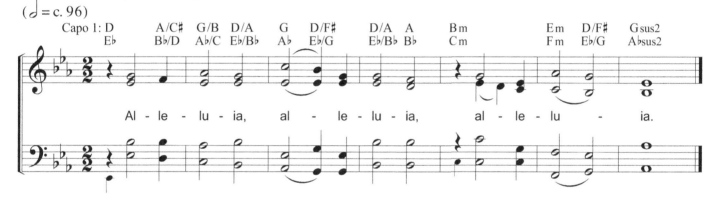

Al - le - lu - ia, al - le - lu - ia, al - le - lu - ia.

Verse: (Cantor) *to Refrain*

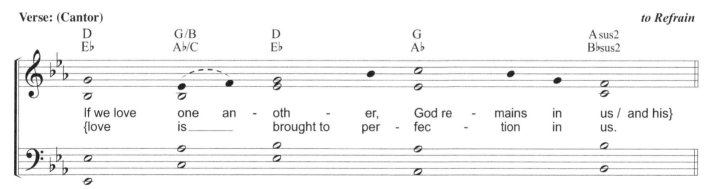

If we love one an - oth - er, God re - mains in us / and his}
{love is _____ brought to per - fec - tion in us.

28th Sunday in Ordinary Time

October 13

Psalm 90:12–13, 14–15, 16–17

(M.M. ♩ = c. 100)

REFRAIN

Fill us with your love, O Lord, and we will sing for joy!

Verses: (Cantor)

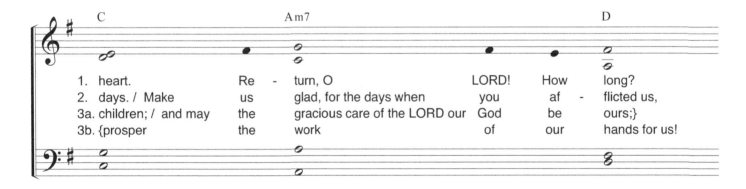

1. Teach us to number our days a - right, that we may gain wis - dom of
2. Fill us at daybreak with your kindness, that we may shout for joy and gladness all our
3. Let your work be seen by your servants and your glory by their

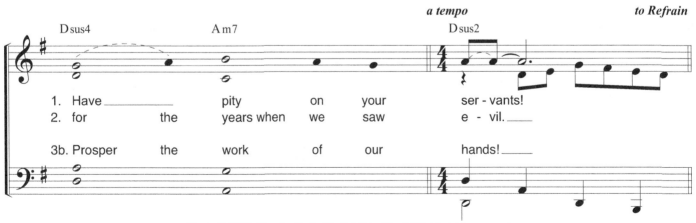

1. heart. Re - turn, O LORD! How long?
2. days. / Make us glad, for the days when you af - flicted us,
3a. children; / and may the gracious care of the LORD our God be ours;}
3b. {prosper the work of our hands for us!

a tempo   *to Refrain*

1. Have _____ pity on your ser - vants!
2. for the years when we saw e - vil. _____

3b. Prosper the work of our hands! _____

Gospel Acclamation: Matthew 5:3
Acclamation: (Keyboard/SATB) NO. III

Al - le - lu - ia, al - le - lu - ia.

Verse: (Cantor)

Blessed are the poor in spirit, / for theirs is the king - dom of heaven.

29th Sunday in Ordinary Time

October 20

(M.M. ♩ = c. 136)

REFRAIN

Psalm 33:4-5, 18-19, 20, 22

Refrain text:
Lord, let your mer-cy be on _____ as we place our trust in you. _____

Verses: (Cantor)

1. (—) Upright is the word of the LORD, / and all his works _____ are trust-worthy. He loves justice and right;
2. See, the eyes of the LORD are up-on those who fear him, / upon those who hope for his kind-ness, / to de-liv-er them from death
3. (—) Our soul _____ waits for the LORD, / who is our help and our shield. _____ / May your kindness, O LORD, be up-on us

1. of the kindness of the LORD the earth is full.
2. and pre - serve them in spite of fam - ine.
3. who have put our hope in you.

Gospel Acclamation: Mark 10:45

Acclamation: (Keyboard/SATB) NO. V

(M.M. ♪ = c. 150)

Al - le - lu - ia, al - le - lu - ia. Al - le - lu - ia, al - le - lu - ia.

Verse: (Cantor) *to Refrain*

The Son of Man came to serve / and to give his life as a ran - som for many.

30th Sunday in Ordinary Time

October 27

Psalm 126:1-2, 2-3, 4-5, 6

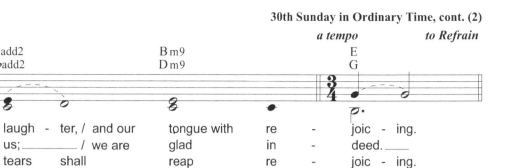

1. filled with laugh - ter, / and our tongue with re - joic - ing.
2. done great things for us; _____ / we are glad in - deed. _____
3. sow in tears shall reap re - joic - ing.
4. back re - joic - ing, carrying their sheaves.

Gospel Acclamation: cf. 2 Timothy 1:10

Acclamation: (Keyboard/SATB) NO. IV

Al - le - lu - ia, _____ al - le - lu - ia, _____ al - le - lu - ia. ia.

Verse: (Cantor) *to Refrain*

Our Savior Je - sus Christ de - stroyed death and brought life to light through the Gospel.

All Saints

November 1

Psalm 24:1bc-2, 3-4ab, 5-6

Gospel Acclamation: Matthew 11:28

Acclamation: (Keyboard/SATB) NO. I

(M.M. ♩ = c. 96)

Verse: (Cantor)

to Refrain

Come to me, all you who labor   and are burdened, / and I will give   you rest, says the Lord.

31st Sunday in Ordinary Time

November 3

Through composed version in *Blessed Assurance* songbook Ed. 10747 available at www.ocp.org.

Gospel Acclamation: John 14:23

Acclamation: (Keyboard/SATB) NO. II

(M.M. ♩ = c. 130)

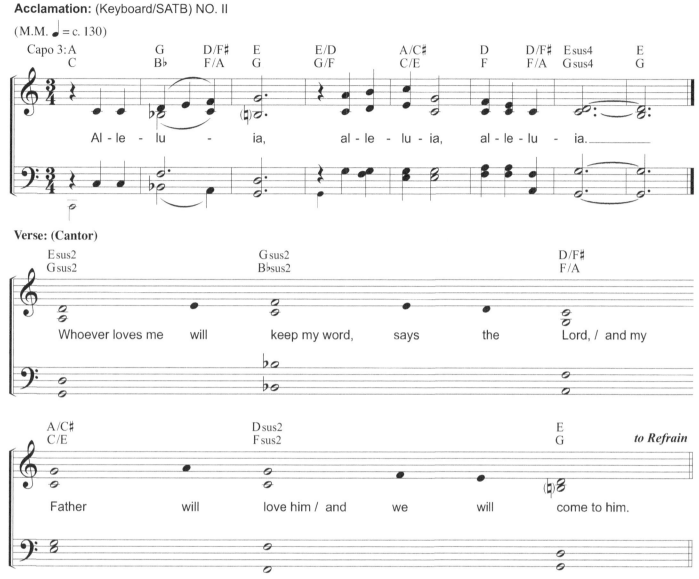

Verse: (Cantor)

Whoever loves me will keep my word, says the Lord, / and my
Father will love him / and we will come to him.

to Refrain

Music © 2014, Timothy R. Smith. Published by TR TUNE, LLC. All rights reserved.

32nd Sunday in Ordinary Time

November 10

Psalm 146:7, 8-9, 9-10

(M.M. ♩ = c. 120)

REFRAIN [or: Alleluia]

Gospel Acclamation: Matthew 5:3
Acclamation: (Keyboard/SATB) NO. III

33rd Sunday in Ordinary Time

November 17

Psalm 16:5, 8, 9-10, 11

Verses: *(Cantor)*

1. O LORD, my al - lot - ted portion and my cup, you it is who
2. Therefore my heart is glad and my soul re - joices, / my bod - y, too, a -
3. You will show me the path to life, full - ness of

1. hold fast my lot. I set the LORD ev - er be -
2. bides in confidence; / because you will not a - bandon my soul to the
3. joys in your presence, / the de - lights at your right hand for -

1. fore me; with him at my right hand I shall not be dis - turbed.
2. netherworld, nor will you suffer your faithful one to undergo cor - rup-tion.
3. ever, / [for – (--) ev-er.]

Gospel Acclamation: Luke 21:36
Acclamation: (Keyboard/SATB) NO. I

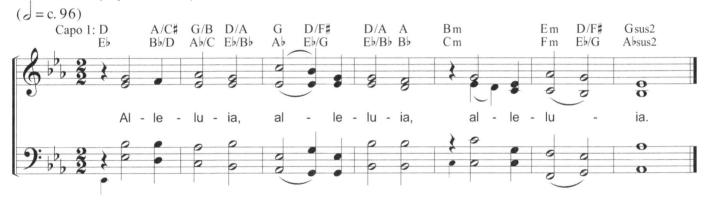

Al - le - lu - ia, al - le - lu - ia, al - le - lu - ia.

Verse: (Cantor)   *to Refrain*

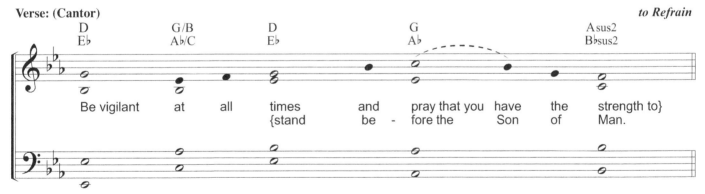

Be vigilant at all times and pray that you have the strength to}
{stand be - fore the Son of Man.

Our Lord Jesus Christ, King of the Universe

November 24

(M.M. ♩ = c. 72)

Psalm 93:1, 1-2, 5

REFRAIN

The Lord is king; he is robed in maj - est - y.

Verses: (Cantor)

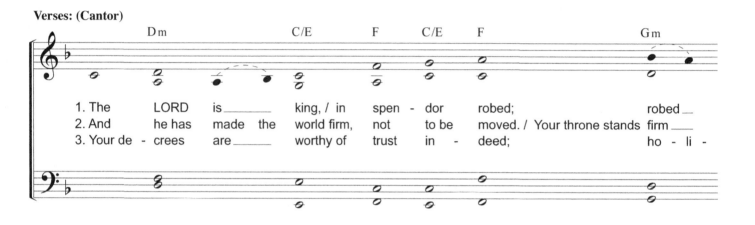

1. The LORD is king, / in spen - dor robed; robed
2. And he has made the world firm, not to be moved. / Your throne stands firm
3. Your de - crees are worthy of trust in - deed; ho - li -

a tempo   *to Refrain*

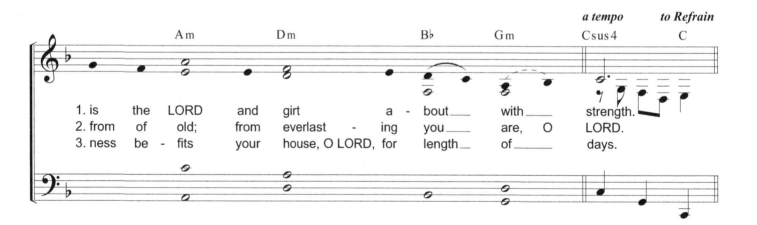

1. is the LORD and girt a - bout with strength.
2. from of old; from everlast - ing you are, O LORD.
3. ness be - fits your house, O LORD, for length of days.

Gospel Acclamation: Mark 11:9,10

Acclamation: (Keyboard/SATB) NO. V

(M.M. ♪ = c. 150)

Al - le -lu - ia, al -le-lu - ia. Al - le -lu - ia, al - le -lu - ia.

Verse: (Cantor) *to Refrain*

Blessed is he who comes in the name of the Lord!}
{Bless - ed is_____ the_____ kingdom of our fath - er David that is to come!

Thanksgiving Day
November 28

For alternate **Responsorial Psalms**, see *Lectionary for the Mass, Second Typical Edition* #945.

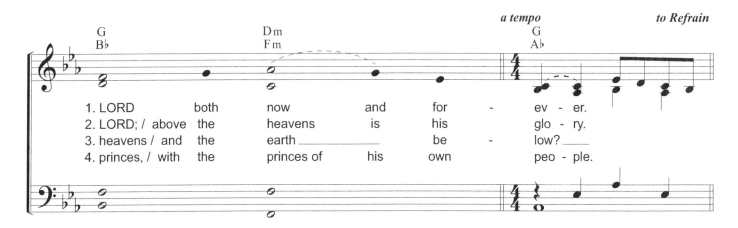

1. LORD both now and for - ev - er.
2. LORD; / above the heavens is his glo - ry.
3. heavens / and the earth _____ be - low? _____
4. princes, / with the princes of his own peo - ple.

Gospel Acclamation: 1 Thessalonians 5:18

Acclamation: (Keyboard/SATB) NO. II

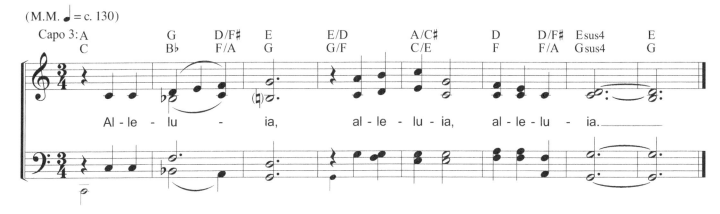

Al - le - lu - ia, al - le - lu - ia, al - le - lu - ia. _____

Verse: (Cantor) *to Refrain*

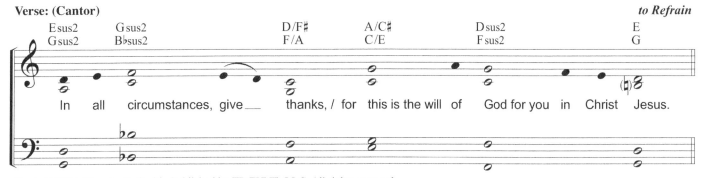

In all circumstances, give _____ thanks, / for this is the will of God for you in Christ Jesus.

For alternate **Gospel Acclamation Verses**, see *Lectionary for the Mass, Second Typical Edition* #946.

Rite of Entrance into the Order of Catechumens

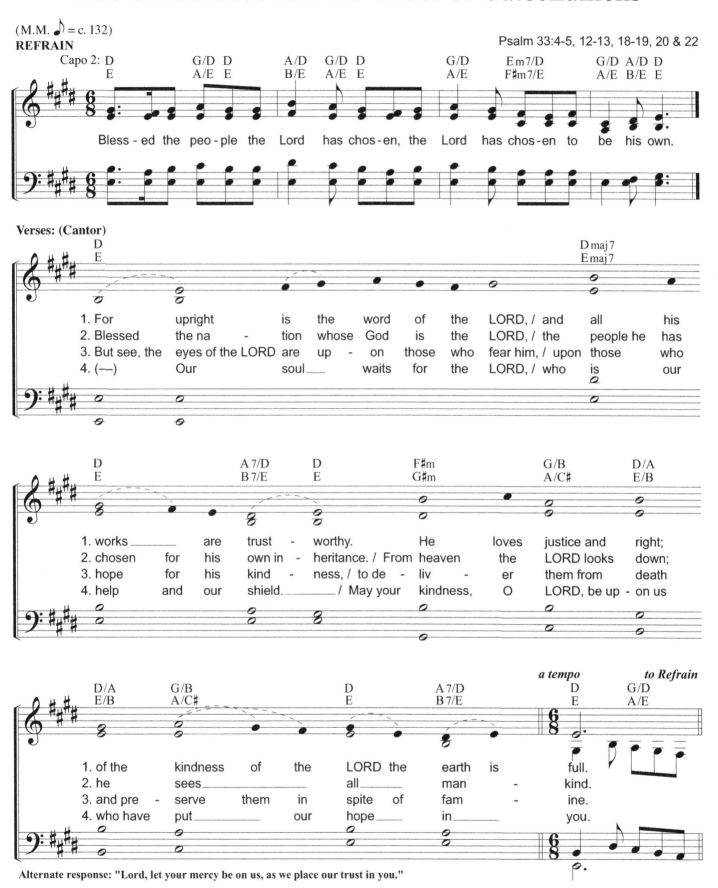

Psalm 33:4-5, 12-13, 18-19, 20 & 22

(M.M. ♪ = c. 132)
REFRAIN

Bless-ed the peo-ple the Lord has chos-en, the Lord has chos-en to be his own.

Verses: (Cantor)

1. For upright is the word of the LORD, / and all his
2. Blessed the na - tion whose God is the LORD, / the people he has
3. But see, the eyes of the LORD are up - on those who fear him, / upon those who
4. (—) Our soul___ waits for the LORD, / who is our

1. works___ are trust - worthy. He loves justice and right;
2. chosen for his own in - heritance. / From heaven the LORD looks down;
3. hope for his kind - ness, / to de - liv - er them from death
4. help and our shield.___ / May your kindness, O LORD, be up - on us

1. of the kindness of the LORD the earth is full.
2. he sees___ all___ man - kind.
3. and pre - serve them in spite of fam - ine.
4. who have put___ our hope___ in___ you.

Alternate response: "Lord, let your mercy be on us, as we place our trust in you."

Gospel Acclamation: John 1:41, 17b

Acclamation: (Keyboard/SATB) NO. V

Al - le-lu - ia, al -le-lu - ia. Al - le-lu - ia, al - le - lu - ia.

We have found the Mes - si - ah: Je - sus Christ, through whom came truth and grace.

Selected Psalm for Weddings

Psalm 128:1-2, 3, 4-5

Alternate Response: "See how the Lord blesses those who fear him."

For alternate **Responsorial Psalms** for weddings, see *Lectionary for the Mass, Second Typical Edition* #803.

Selected Psalm for Funerals

Alternate response: "The salvation of the just comes from the Lord."

For alternate **Responsorial Psalms** for funerals, see *Lectionary for the Mass, Second Typical Edition* #1013.

Selected Common (Seasonal) Psalm for Ordinary Time

(M.M. ♩ = c. 72)

REFRAIN

Psalm 27:1, 4, 13-14

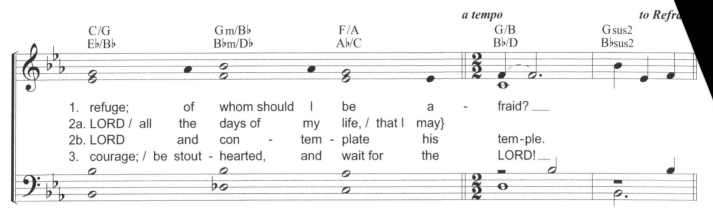

1. refuge; of whom should I be a - fraid? ___
2a. LORD / all the days of my life, / that I may}
2b. LORD and con - tem - plate his tem-ple.
3. courage; / be stout - hearted, and wait for the LORD! ___

Made in the USA
Columbia, SC
12 June 2023

17806894R00098